FamilyTime

A Collection of 98
Bible Stories and Devotions

Bible Story Devotions

Special Occasion Devotions

© 2014 Concordia Publishing House
3558 S. Jefferson Avenue, St. Louis, MO 63118-3968
1-800-325-3040 • www.cph.org

Edited by Rodney L. Rathmann and Carolyn Bergt

Assisted by Barbara Szofran and Johanna Saleska

Artwork © Concordia Publishing House/Michelle Dorenkamp Repa and Jeff Albrecht

Unless otherwise indicated, Scripture quotations are from the ESV Bible®
(The Holy Bible, English Standard Version®), copyright © 2001 by Crossway Bibles,
a publishing ministry of Good News Publishers. Used by permission. All rights
reserved.

Abbreviation *LSB* refers to *Lutheran Service Book*, copyright © 2006 Concordia
Publishing House. All rights reserved.

Manufactured in HeShan, China/047365/407015

1 2 3 4 5 6 7 8 9 10   22 21 20 19 18 17 16 15 14 13

Being a parent can be one of life's greatest joys. But it also brings with it a set of awesome responsibilities and challenges. Unfortunately, parenting seems to demand so much from us at just the time of life when so much else demands heavily of our time, efforts, and creative energies.

Spending time with your child reading, hearing, and discussing God's Word brings big results. We are reminded in 1 Timothy 4:8 that "while bodily training is of some value, godliness is of value in every way, as it holds promise for the present life and also for the life to come."

We train our children in godliness when we introduce them to Jesus, our Savior and theirs, and when we talk to them in a natural, conversational way about spiritual things. Training children in godliness is not beyond the reach of anyone wanting to be a good parent. Reading and discussing God's Word together as a family can be an important part of growing together as a family.

This book has been especially designed to help you spend time with God as a family each day. It provides a series of devotions for families with growing children.

The devotions in this book are organized in two groupings. The first set of devotions answers questions about the Christian faith and what it means to live for Jesus while referencing Bible stories presented in chronological order. The second set provides devotions for special times, such as holidays or when experiencing life events such as the birth of a sibling or the death of a family member or pet (see the index in the back of the book).

You may choose to go through the devotions in this book two or more times. The first time, you may read and discuss the Bible story. The second time, you may want to read and reflect on the devotion. Or you may choose to do a combination of both. Be sure to draw attention to the Bible words and corresponding Christian teaching found on each two-page spread.

The important thing is to spend time together in talking about God and what He tells us in His Word. Feel free to read all or only portions of these devotions as time allows.

Close with a short prayer. Remember to keep devotion and prayer time short, as young children have very short attention spans. Watch your children for clues that will be helpful in pacing the devotion time.

Your role will be to read from God's Word and the devotion and lead the discussion. Share what Jesus means to you. Tell your children stories from your life or the lives of others in your family to help them understand God's saving, forgiving power as it has come down through all generations.

Trust in God as you lead family devotion time. Through His Word, God Himself will do the teaching; He promises to work the results. Isaiah 54:13 reminds us, "All your children shall be taught by the Lord, and great shall be the peace of your children."

But to all who did receive Him, who believed in His name,
He gave the right to become children of God. John 1:12

Jesus Has the Words of Eternal Life | John 6:66–69

Long ago, God sent His Son to earth to save all people from their sins. God named His Son Jesus. Jesus was born in a tiny town called Bethlehem, but He grew up in the home of His parents, Mary and Joseph, in the town of Nazareth. When Jesus was a young man, He gathered around Him a group of followers. These followers were called disciples. There were twelve of them, and their names were Peter, Andrew, James the son of Zebedee, John, Philip, Bartholomew, Thomas, Matthew, James the son of Alphaeus, Thaddaeus, Simon the Zealot, and Judas Iscariot.

Jesus taught many things. Some of the things He taught were hard to understand. Some of those who heard Jesus' teachings turned away. They no longer wanted to follow Him. Jesus asked His twelve disciples, "Do you want to go away as well?" Peter, one of the twelve, answered Him, "Lord, to whom shall we go? You have the words of eternal life, and we have believed, and have come to know, that You are the Holy One of God." By these words, Peter showed that he believed in Jesus as the Son of God and Savior of the world. Today, those who believe in Jesus as Peter did are His disciples too.

Who Are You? / Isaiah 43:1

Boys and girls sometimes said Wilson Taylor was lucky. "Wilson, you have two last names!" they said. In the same neighborhood, there lived the Tim family. The boys and girls in the neighborhood said Andy Tim was lucky too. "Andy, you have two first names!" they said.

Most of us have two names. We have our first name, the name our parents gave us when we were born. And we have a last name, the name of our family. Not only do people have names, but animals and plants have names too. There are also many names for God.

Jesus is God. He is often called by two names: Jesus Christ. *Jesus* means "Savior." Jesus came to save all people from their sins. *Christ* means "promised one." Jesus was promised to Adam and Eve shortly after they listened to the devil and sinned by disobeying God.

People who know and believe in Jesus as their Savior and follow Him are called Christians. If you believe in Jesus as your Savior, that's a name that you can be called as well.

Talk about it: What other names do we have because of Jesus? (Christian, child of God, disciple, believer)

Thank You, dear Savior, for making me Your child by taking away my sins. Thank You for the privilege of being a Christian, a member of Your family in faith. Keep me in the faith and help me always to live for You. In Jesus' name I pray. Amen.

But these are written so that you may believe that Jesus is the Christ, the Son of God. John 20:31

John Writes about Jesus | John 20:30–31

John was one of Jesus' followers. As a disciple of Jesus, John followed Jesus and learned from Him. When soldiers took Jesus to die on the cross for the sins of the world, John stood at the foot of the cross together with Jesus' mother. After Jesus died, His followers placed His body into a tomb. But Jesus didn't stay dead. He came back to life. After Jesus rose from the dead, John came to see the empty tomb. Later, John was together with the other disciples when Jesus appeared before them. Finally, John was present when Jesus ascended, rising up from the earth to go into heaven.

Years later, John wrote down all that happened. He wrote that Jesus is God, who created the world. He wrote about what Jesus taught about God's love and the people He healed when He walked the earth. John wrote about Jesus suffering and dying and rising again from the dead to pay for your sins and my sins and the sins of all people. John wrote many words, but John didn't write on His own. John wrote the very words God gave Him to write. John said this about the words he wrote: "These are written so that you may believe that Jesus is the Christ, the Son of God, and that by believing you may have life in His name."

The Bible is made up of sixty-six separate writings. John's writings and those of many other people are found in the Bible. Still, all the words in the Bible are really the words of God, because God told all the writers of the Bible the words to write. The Bible has one main message: Jesus is the Son of God and Savior of the world.

The Story of God, the Story of Us / 2 Timothy 3:15

Caleb loved family holiday dinners. Everybody got together around the big dining room table. Lots of talk and teasing went on over a big meal. His grandparents told stories about when his mom and dad were little. His aunts and uncles told about the fun they had together as kids.

Caleb and his cousins knew most of the stories by heart. Still, they were eager to hear them again and again. "Grandpa," Caleb begged, "tell about the time Dad climbed the tree and couldn't get down." And Grandpa would smile, lean back in his chair, and begin the story once more.

The Bible tells the story of God's family. It tells how God created us and made us His own. It contains stories about people depending on God to send a Savior. Noah, Joseph, and Daniel are just a few. Knowing how God kept them strong gives us courage.

The Bible tells us God's plan and promises. Even when mankind fell into sin, God loved us. He sent Jesus to take the punishment for us by dying on a cross. Jesus' death and resurrection give us eternal life. That's a story worth knowing!

Keeping these stories in our hearts helps us remember that we are God's family. And we can share our family stories with others. That will remind believers of God's saving power. It will show unbelievers what God has done for us and for all people. If we tell the stories, everyone can know God's love and salvation.

Talk about it: What is one of your favorite Bible stories? (Possibilities include Noah and the flood, Joseph's colorful coat, Daniel in the lions' den, the good Samaritan, and the resurrection.)

Prayer: Lord God, let me never get tired of reading, studying, and learning Your Word. Amen.

God Creates the World and Us | Genesis 1:1—2:3

Nothing. Nothing at all. God made heaven and earth from nothing. It was very dark, so God made light. He called the light "day." The dark was "night." This was the first day and night!

God was busy the second day too. Water was everywhere, so God made the sky. It was pretty and blue. What would God make on the third day?

God made dry ground. He called the dry ground "land." He called the water "seas." Then God made plants for the land.

Now it was day four. God made lights for the sky. The sun would give light to the earth and make flowers grow. God also placed stars and the moon in the sky.

God made water animals and sky animals next. On day five, God made so much to enjoy.

More animals! God made more animals to live on the land. God made them all on day six. And He did more! God made people in a special way. First, God made Adam, forming him out of the dust of the ground. Then, later, God caused Adam to fall asleep. God took a rib from Adam, and from this rib, God made Eve. Adam and Eve were the first people on the earth. God put them in charge of all He made. They were happy. All the animals were friendly. God made everything very good.

God rested on day seven. The work was done! Our God is great!

God made a wonderful, beautiful world. Even though it is no longer as wonderful as it was before the coming of sin, God's creation is still awesome and amazing. God still loves everything He has made. Soon after the first sin entered the world, God promised to send His only Son to save all people and to earn forgiveness for their sins.

Work of Art / Psalm 33:6–9

Have you ever been to an art museum? If so, you've probably noticed all the different types of art on display. Some paintings are incredibly detailed, while others appear to be no more than paint splatters on a canvas. Some use many colors; some use few colors. Sculptures can be marble, clay, granite, or even papier-mâché. All the different types and styles of art make going to the art museum fun and unique. The variety keeps the museum from getting boring.

You could say that God is the best, most famous artist there ever was. He created the beauty of the earth, the sea, and the sky. He spoke into being the sun, moon, and all the planets. He molded Adam from the dust of the ground, and then he sculpted Eve from Adam's rib bone. Every person who has ever existed belongs to God. Even before we are born, God knows us. Not only does He know us, but He also has a plan and purpose for our lives.

Look at all the people around you. You may not like everyone you meet. But God loves every one of the people He has made. He sent His beloved Son, Jesus Christ, to die for all humankind, so that we might have victory over sin and the gift of eternal life.

The art gallery of life is filled with living masterpieces, created and re-created by God Himself, and you are one of the most beautiful masterpieces of all!

Talk about it: How are you special and wonderfully made? What are some unique features that God gave you?

Heavenly Father, what a wonderful, beautiful world You have made! Be with me as I experience Your creation, especially all the people around me. Thank You for Your love and forgiveness in Jesus Christ. Amen.

13

Adam and Eve Sin | Genesis 2–3

God made the world and everything in it. He took only six days to do it! He made the earth, sky, and water. He made every plant and animal. He made the first people. God formed a man named Adam from the dust of the ground. Adam named all the animals. None of the animals were made like Adam. He was lonely, so God made a woman named Eve to live with Adam. They lived in a beautiful garden called Eden. Adam and Eve were happy in the garden. They took care of the plants and animals. Adam and Eve loved God. They loved each other.

God gave Adam and Eve one rule: not to eat fruit from the tree in the center of the garden. God said, "Do not eat from it or you will die." We call the things God wants us to do *God's Law*.

One day, the devil came to Eve in the shape of a snake. He told Eve not to believe God. He told her the fruit would make her be like God. Eve listened to the snake. She disobeyed God and sinned. She ate the fruit and gave some to Adam. He ate it and sinned too. This was the first sin. Adam and Eve suddenly became aware that they had done wrong; they tried to hide from God. Forever after that first sin, when they and all people measured themselves against the expectations of God's Law, they would find themselves lacking and imperfect.

But God does not leave us in our sin. When we repent, He showers us with the forgiveness and salvation Jesus earned for us by keeping God's Law perfectly in our place and by taking upon Himself the punishment we deserved.

Now, as His forgiven people, we look upon God's Law in yet another way. We desire to do God's will and allow God's will to guide us through the new life God has given us—a life lived for Him.

Night Hike

[...] and Actual / 1 John 3:8

Barbara and her friends were fully prepared for their hike through the forest. At the last minute, they decided to throw a few flashlights in their backpacks. They didn't think they'd need them. It was only mid-afternoon, and the path they had chosen wasn't supposed to take more than a few hour[s] But the flashlights were [...] to carry, and it wouldn't [...] and bring them just in c[...]

The path led th[...] sharp and along a gurglin[...] only way to stream. The th[...] ve the area. surrounded t[...] is a good name lowed the tr[...] He goes unno- and up an[...] ting here and there. The bric[...] schools and tempts descend[...] to cheat on tests. He a coupl[...] round homes and sug- friends[...] hat family members lie get b[...] another. He sneaks into sunse[...]

be caught [...] dark. The [...] thoughts and suggests faster [...] wrong is right and right is ther[...] wrong. s[...]ng.

The devil tempted Adam and Eve many years ago. You know the story. God forbade Adam and Eve from eating the fruit, but they ate it anyway. They sinned. All people since that moment have been born with a sinful condition called original sin. There is no escape from original sin; we all suffer from it. It is part of who we are, in our original human condition.

In addition to this, we also commit actual sins on a regular basis. For example, we might envy others, and our envy can turn to hatred. If we allow our envy and hatred to continue unchecked, as it did when Cain killed Abel, worse and worse sins can result. All sin disconnects us from God. The no-see-um devil bites hard, tempting us, hoping to separate us from God—and he often succeeds.

But God doesn't leave us without help. He comes to us in His Word and in the Sacraments of Holy Baptism and the Lord' Supper. He promises to help us withstand temptation. He changes us into children of God.

Talk about it: The devotion mentions two different kinds of sin: original and actual. What is the difference between these two kinds of sin? Who helps us with our problem of sin? What help does He provide?

Prayer: Our Father, give us strength to resist and overcome temptation. Forgive our sins for Jesus' sake. Amen.

Unless one is born of water and the Spirit, he cannot enter the kingdom of God. John 3:5

God Saves Noah in the Ark | Genesis 6–8

Adam and Eve had children. Their children had children. Soon, the world was filled with people. The people were very wicked. God was very sad that He had made people. He decided to rid the world of the wicked people. But God loved Noah, and Noah loved God. God told Noah to build a big boat called an ark. God would save Noah and his family.

God brought animals into the ark. He brought at least two of every kind. Then Noah went into the boat. Noah's wife, their three sons, and their sons' wives also went into the boat. God closed the door to the ark. Then God sent rain. It rained and rained and rained. At last, the entire earth was covered with water. All the animals and people outside of the ark died. But the animals

and people inside the ark did not die. God kept them safe.

Then God caused the wind to blow. The waters dried up. The ark came to rest on the top of a mountain. The animals and people left the ark. Noah built an altar. He worshiped and praised God. God placed a rainbow in the sky. The rainbow reminds us of God's love and promises.

When God dried the earth, Noah and the animals came out of the ark. They entered a brand-new world, a world cleaned by God with the waters of the flood. The great flood can remind us of our Baptism. In Baptism, God drowns our old sinful nature and calls us into a new life as people of God. Baptism makes us new people and calls us into a new life—a new life in Jesus.

Brand New / 2 Corinthians 5:17

On Sunday morning at the beginning of summer vacation, Jake got up on time and got ready for church. He was happy about going to worship God with other Christians. Jake felt that he was growing and learning and was ready to pay better attention in church.

To his surprise, he saw Abby and Jo at church. They were visiting Abby's grandparents. While they chatted about last year's VBS camp, it was almost like being back there. Then Jake remembered what his teacher had said about how good-bye isn't a final farewell for Christians, but it means going with God, knowing that we'll see other Christians later. It was true!

That afternoon, Jake went to a birthday party. He couldn't believe his eyes. Kyle was there! Jake had met Kyle recently at Sunday School. Kyle's dad worked with Jake's dad. They had fun swimming and made up a game like water polo. The day flew by.

When Jake got home, he told his dad he felt different—almost like he was starting all over. He felt like a new person because he had lots of new friends who really cared about him. These new friends also loved Jesus and shared many of his values.

Jake's dad said there is even more good news. God makes each person new in Baptism, allowing us to live a new life in Christ each day. Jake's dad then reminded him that VBS started on Monday. At first, Jake thought he was too old for VBS. He had begged his dad not to make him go. Now, Jake looked forward to making more new Christian friends. In Christ, all things are new—even the way we see others—as we live with brothers and sisters in Christ.

Talk about it: Describe how it feels to be new in Christ.

Prayer: Dear God, thanks for making me new in Christ Jesus through Baptism. Give me Your Spirit's power so that I might see today's activities with new eyes. Amen.

The Tower of Babel | Genesis 11:1–9

After the world's great flood, Noah's children had many children, and these children had many children, until the world had many people once again. At this time, all the people in the world spoke one language. The people traveled east until they found a plain in the land of Shinar, and they stayed there.

They said, "Let's make bricks and build a city and a tower whose top will reach to the heavens; and let's make a name for ourselves in this place rather than spreading out all over the world."

God knew the proud and wicked plans of the people. He said, "The people are united with one language, and they have wicked, prideful plans. Let Us give them many languages so that they will not understand one another." And so it happened that work on the tower and the city stopped, and the people spread out over all the earth. The place where God caused the people to speak many languages became known as Babel.

Doing It His Way / Isaiah 55:6–9

It was a windy fall day. Marty fingered his rake as he watched the last of the leaves float onto the brownish lawn. His father had told him to rake the leaves in the direction the wind was blowing and had left him a pair of gloves. But Marty didn't need anyone else to do his thinking for him. He decided to rake the leaves the other way—against the wind. And gloves were for sissies!

For an hour, Marty raked furiously. He had built a large pile of leaves, but many more had escaped his rake in the steady wind. As Marty walked into the garage to get bags to hold his pile of leaves, he noticed the large blisters that were forming on his hands. One had already broken and stung quite a lot. Marty began to regret doing things his own way.

"I want to do it my way." How often have we heard—or said—those words? In the Garden of Eden, Adam and Eve wanted to do things their way. Later, the world was filled with so much wickedness and people doing whatever they wanted that God destroyed everything except for Noah, his family, and the animals with them in the ark. Later still, God commanded the people to spread out over the earth. But they wanted to do things their own way instead. Instead of obeying God, they set out to build a tall tower to make a name for themselves.

People wanting to do things their own way did not stop with the tower of Babel. We want to do things our own way today too. Whenever we do things motivated by our selfishness, we sin. We reject God's way of doing things.

But God had a plan to make His way our way again. He sent His Son as our Savior. Jesus lived His life God's way. He didn't sin, even though He was tempted many times. He paid for our sins—all the times we have gone against God's way—on the cross. He made us right in God's eyes. And for eternity, God's way will be our way.

Talk about it: What happens when we do things our own way? How does God make His way our way?

Prayer: Help us remember Your way in everything we do, Lord. Guide us by Your Spirit so that the way we choose may be pleasing to You. Amen.

For My thoughts are not your thoughts, neither are your ways
My ways, declares the LORD. Isaiah 55:8

Abraham Offers Isaac as a Sacrifice | Genesis 22:1–18

After God separated the people according to their language groups, people again began to worship idols and to do other things that disobeyed God. But God told a man named Abraham and his wife, Sarah, to move away from the people who worshiped idols and to go to a land God would give them. Abraham followed God's directions. He moved to the land of Canaan. When Abraham and Sarah were both old, God gave them a son, Isaac. Abraham was 100 years old when Isaac was born.

Later, God told Abraham to go with Isaac to the land of Moriah and offer him there as a sacrifice. Abraham obeyed. Getting up early one morning, he saddled his donkey and left, taking with him two servants, Isaac, and some wood. On the third day of this journey, Abraham saw Moriah in the distance. Leaving the servants with the donkey, he set off with Isaac on foot. Isaac carried the wood for the sacrifice while Abraham carried the fire and a knife. As they traveled, Isaac asked, "Father, we have fire and wood, but where is the lamb for the sacrifice?"

Abraham replied, "God Himself will provide a lamb for the sacrifice." Upon reaching their destination, Abraham built an altar and laid the wood upon it. Then he tied Isaac and placed him on the wood and lifted his knife over Isaac.

At that moment, the Angel of the Lord called from heaven, saying, "Abraham, do not lay a hand on the boy; for now I know that you love Me greatly, since you would not even withhold your only son from Me." Then Abraham saw a ram caught in a thicket by his horns. He went and took the ram and offered it up for a burnt offering instead of Isaac. The angel reminded Abraham of God's promise that many descendants would be born to him, including the Savior of the world. Abraham and Isaac returned to their home. Abraham simply trusted God and followed His directions, and God blessed him. (Note that God Himself did not spare His only begotten Son but sacrificed Him on the cross to redeem the world because of His great love.)

God's Directions / Psalm 16:11

Joel's family was moving from Pennsylvania to California. At first, Joel wasn't 100 percent sure that he wanted to move. He would miss his friends, his school, and his house. But the more the family talked about it and planned, the more excited he became. He even made a list of good things about his new home:

- Close to the beach
- No snow to shovel
- Disneyland an hour away
- New friends

One thing that made Joel feel better was that his whole family had prayed about the move. They prayed that God would show them where to live, when to move, and even what route to take to California. After the prayers, they made lists, looked at maps, and planned everything for their big mission.

Sometimes, you may face things that you don't want to do. It's okay to ask God for another way. Sometimes, He may show you another way. Other times, you will know that you have to follow the path God has put in front of you. Take comfort in knowing that God is at your side. We can trust in God and we can trust that things will always work out for the best because we belong to Him.

Talk about it: When have you wondered about something God allowed to come into your life? What good thing might God bring to you as a result?

Prayer: Dear heavenly Father, I'm so glad You made me Your own dear child through Jesus' sacrifice. Help me always to trust in You. Help me always to follow You. I pray in Jesus' name. Amen.

It is not good that the man should be alone;
I will make him a helper fit for him. Genesis 2:18

Isaac Marries Rebekah | Genesis 24

God promised Abraham and Sarah that the Savior of the world would be born as one of their descendants. When Isaac, their son, had grown up, Abraham worried that Isaac would marry a woman who did not believe in the true God. So Abraham sent his servant to his hometown to find a wife for Isaac. Abraham's servant prayed that God would show him the woman who would be a good wife for Isaac. A young woman offered Abraham's servant a drink of water and offered to water his camels too. The servant knew that God had chosen this woman, Rebekah, for Isaac.

Rebekah took the servant to meet her family. The servant gave them gifts from Abraham. When he told Rebekah and her family the reason for his visit, Rebekah's family knew this was from the Lord. Rebekah returned with the servant to marry Isaac, and Isaac loved her.

According to God's Plan / Ephesians 5:4

Amy dreamed about growing up and getting married. She dreamed of wearing a beautiful dress and standing before God's altar with her husband, promising to live together and love each other for the rest of their lives. She was thrilled by movies where this seemed to happen.

Whether we grow up and get married, or whether we remain single all our lives, God has a plan for each of us. He desires us to honor Him in the way we think about ourselves and our bodies. He wants us to honor and respect all other people too.

God also wants us to show honor and respect for the way He wants us to live. We serve God in this way by thinking and speaking about only clean and decent subjects.

When we think about living a decent life, we can think about Jesus. Because Jesus is also fully human, He was tempted to think and speak and do wrong things just as we are.

Because Jesus is God, He did not sin. He came to earn forgiveness for all the wrong things we do. Whether we grow up and marry someone or whether we remain single, we do not go through life alone. Jesus promises always to remain with us. He will forgive us our sins and bless us with His unending love.

~~~~~~~~~~~~~~~~~~

Talk about it: Would you like to get married someday? Why or why not? Give an example of how God leads your life today.

Prayer: Heavenly Father, You have created us as boys and girls, men and women. Help us to live and serve You all our life in all we are and do. Thank You for the love and forgiveness we have in Jesus. We pray in His name. Amen.

Fear not, for I am with you; be not dismayed,
for I am your God;
I will strengthen you, I will help you,
I will uphold you with
My righteous right hand. Isaiah 41:10

Jacob's Dream | Genesis 27–28

Isaac and Rebekah became the parents of two sons, Jacob and Esau. Jacob cheated Esau and tricked his father, Isaac. Esau became very angry. So Jacob had to leave home. Their mother, Rebekah, thought Jacob would be safe at his uncle's house in another country.

The trip was long. Soon it was night. Jacob stopped to get some sleep. He used a rock for a pillow. Jacob was very tired. He fell into a deep sleep and began to dream. God sent the dream to Jacob.

In his dream, Jacob saw a ladder. The bottom of the ladder rested on the earth. The top reached into heaven. Angels were walking up and down the ladder. God had a message for Jacob. God said, "I will give you the land on which you are sleeping. It will belong to your children and your grandchildren. I will make you and your family very special. I will bless all people because of your family."

Jacob woke up. He knew he had been close to God. He used his stone pillow to mark the place where he slept. He named the place Bethel, which means "the House of God." Jacob knew he was safe. Jacob then went on to his uncle's house.

This dream had a special meaning for Jacob. As surely as God forgave Jacob, He promised to remain with him and to continue His blessings upon Jacob and his family. Many years after Jacob lived, Jesus, the Savior, was born into this family.

Of Sin and Consequences, Love and Hope / 1 Peter 4:8

Pam looked over her shoulder. No one was around. She quietly opened the garage door and wheeled out her brother's bike. Her bike was old, but Mark's bike was shiny and new. I'm almost safe, she thought.

"Hi, Pam" called Mrs. Thorton. "How are you today?"

"Just fine," Pam answered with a nervous glance at the house. She hoped Dad hadn't heard the neighbor. Right then, Dad walked around the corner of the garage. Pam's stomach dropped.

He looked disappointed. "What are you doing?" he asked.

"I'm sorry, Dad," said Pam, feeling a little nauseous. "I

wouldn't hurt Mark's bike. Honest."

"That's not the point, and you know it," said Dad. "You disobeyed me. You were not to take Mark's bike, or what would happen?"

Pam hung her head. She couldn't bear to look at Dad. "You said I wouldn't be able to go anywhere for a week." Now Pam faced punishment.

The Bible tells us that because of sin, all of us deserve the punishment of death. In other words, because we all break God's Commandments, all of us deserve to go to hell. That's a scary thought. Thankfully, the Bible also gives us hope. God's gift to us is eternal life in heav-

en, not because of anything we have done, but because of His Son's death on our behalf. Jesus lived a perfect life; He never broke even one commandment. Jesus died in our place and rose again for us! Plus, because Jesus loves us and has forgiven us, He promises always to remain with us and never to leave us. He loves us that much!

Talk about it: When have you done something wrong and received a punishment? Can you think of a time when you did not get punished as you deserved? What can we always remember about Jesus when we feel sorry over a sin we have committed? when we feel alone?

Prayer: Dear Savior, thank You for Your great love and mercy. Thank You for promising always to remain with me and never to leave me. Forgive my sins. Keep my faith strong in You. Amen.

Everyone who hates his brother is a murderer, and you know that no murderer has eternal life abiding in him. 1 John 3:15

Joseph's Special Coat | Genesis 37

Jacob came to live at his uncle's home. While there, he married and had many children. Joseph was Jacob's favorite son. Jacob treated Joseph better than he treated his eleven other sons. Jacob gave Joseph a beautiful robe. There was no other like it. Joseph's brothers were jealous and hated Joseph.

Joseph had some dreams. He told them to his family. But the dreams made his brothers hate him even more. Joseph dreamed that his brothers bowed down to him. Joseph's second dream was like his first. This time, even the sun, moon, and stars bowed down to him.

The brothers planned to kill Joseph. But the brother named Reuben wanted to rescue Joseph. Another brother, Judah, said they should sell him.

So they sold Joseph to some slave traders. Joseph was only seventeen years old at the time.

The brothers did not want to tell their father what they had done. They planned to trick him. They put goat's blood on Joseph's pretty robe. Jacob thought a wild animal had killed Joseph, but Joseph was alive. The slave traders sold Joseph to a man in Egypt. The brothers' hatred of Joseph led them to speak and do other bad things. They hurt Joseph in many ways because they hated him. But God had good plans for Joseph. God would always be with Joseph. Joseph would see his family again. He would forgive his brothers. God's love for us in Jesus helps us to love and forgive those who hate and hurt us just as Joseph did.

Friends Again / Ephesians 4:32

Marcie and Jack were class-mates. Each tried to outdo the other, and sometimes they got carried away. One day, Marcie saw a chance to get the upper hand. Jack had messed up big-time, and Marcie let him know it.

"Jack," she exclaimed, "you're a terrible excuse for a human being! Even God doesn't love you."

As she turned to flee, Marcie ran right into her pastor, who was walking through the hallway of their Christian school. "Pastor!" she said. "How are you?"

"Marcie," he replied, "I heard you. How could you say what you said?" Marcie's red cheeks suddenly reddened with embarrassment. Then she said simply, "I'm sorry."

Pastor said, "Marcie, you're forgiven for Jesus' sake. Now, you know what to do next?"

Marcie didn't want to hear it. She'd "get to" apologize to Jack, promising never to speak that way again. "I can't," Marcie confessed.

"You can," Pastor said, "because the Lord will strengthen you. Pray for that before you go."

Marcie's words to Jack tumbled out slowly and haltingly: "I'm sor–ry . . . for . . . what . . . I . . . said."

Jack thought for a moment and then answered, "I forgive you because Jesus has forgiven me." His quick smile sealed the moment. The rivals were friends again.

~~~~~~~~~~

Talk about it: The Bible says that when we hate someone we break God's commandment "You shall not murder." God does not want us to hurt other people in any way. Think about the last person you wronged with your words or actions. How can God's power change things around? Who needs your forgiveness today?

Prayer: Gracious Father, I know how much You have forgiven me through Your Son, Jesus Christ. Help me forgive those I have wronged, and help us become friends again. For Jesus' sake I pray. Amen.

God is faithful, and He will not let you be tempted beyond your ability, but with the temptation He will also provide the way of escape, that you may be able to endure it. 1 Corinthians 10:13

Joseph in Egypt | Genesis 39–46

Jacob's sons hated their brother Joseph. They sold Joseph as a slave. Then they tricked their father. They dipped Joseph's coat in goat's blood and showed it to Jacob. Jacob thought a wild animal had killed Joseph.

But Joseph was still alive! God was with Joseph in good times and in bad times. In Egypt, the slave traders sold Joseph to a man named Potiphar. Potiphar's wife wanted Joseph to do something that was wrong. She tried to coax him and coax him. She tried to get Joseph to sin, just as the serpent tried to get Adam and Eve to sin long before in the Garden of Eden. But Joseph would not listen. One day, Potiphar's wife told a lie about Joseph, so Potiphar put Joseph into prison. But God blessed Joseph even when he was in jail.

There, Joseph met Pharaoh's butler and baker. The butler and baker both had dreams.

God told Joseph the meaning of their dreams. Then Pharaoh let the butler get out of prison. Later, Pharaoh had a dream. The butler told Pharaoh about Joseph. Pharaoh asked Joseph, "Can you tell me what my dream means?" God told Joseph the meaning of Pharaoh's dream. Pharaoh made Joseph a ruler in Egypt. When Joseph's family was without food, Joseph saved them all by giving them the food they needed.

Joseph forgave his brothers for being mean, and he brought his family to live with him in Egypt. Jesus forgives all that we have done wrong and will bring us to live with Him someday in heaven.

No Slips / Psalm 121

A wet floor, a rocky trail, and a skateboard—what do they have in common? They can threaten our balance and cause us to fall, bringing discomfort, injury, and recuperation time.

Psalm 121:7 says, "The LORD will keep you from all evil." The psalmist knew about temptations, thoughts, and actions that lure us away from God's will. He reminded us that God is always with us and wants to keep us from slipping into sin.

Sometimes, we are all lured away from what is right. We are surrounded by temptations from the devil, the world, and our own sinful flesh. We make poor decisions, or our emotions get the better of us. Sometimes, we choose the easiest way— the path of least resistance.

Sin causes us to slip, but when tempted or in danger we can look to God for His help and guidance. We have His protection in dangerous situations. His Spirit calms our emotions, enabling us to think clearly. His Word promises guidance for the day's struggles and provides light when life's path is rough and twisted.

With the Holy Spirit at our side, we can follow the path of truth and righteousness. With His powerful assistance, we can make God-pleasing decisions that bring peace and joy into our lives.

Have temptations led you to slip into sin lately? Our Savior, Jesus Christ, is there. His death and resurrection assure you of God's forgiveness. The gift of faith grasps God's promise. He will pick you up and give you the peace found only in Him.

Talk about it: What did Joseph do when Potiphar's wife coaxed him to sin? How can God keep you from sin when you face temptations? How can Jesus help when you do slip?

Prayer: Dear Jesus, forgive me when I slip away from You. Send Your Spirit to show me the right path and keep me in Your grace. In Your name I pray. Amen.

You were ransomed from the futile ways inherited from your forefathers, not with perishable things such as silver or gold, but with the precious blood of Christ, like that of a lamb without blemish or spot. 1 Peter 1:18–19

God Saves His People | Exodus 5–14

God was with Joseph and made him a ruler in Egypt. Joseph forgave his brothers and brought his father, Jacob, and his entire family to live in Egypt. Here, they enjoyed a good life and grew in numbers until they became a mighty nation of God's people. But a new king, or Pharaoh, in Egypt became afraid because there were so many of them. So he made them slaves.

In the misery of their slavery, the people cried out to God. God raised up a leader named Moses to lead His people to freedom. Moses went to Pharaoh's palace often. His brother Aaron went with him. They asked Pharaoh to let God's people leave Egypt. Pharaoh refused, so God turned water into blood. He punished Egypt with large numbers of frogs, lice, flies, and locusts. Still, Pharaoh would not let God's people go. God sent sickness, storms, and darkness. Even then, Pharaoh would not free God's people. Then God told Moses to tell the people, "Prepare a lamb for food. Sprinkle the lamb's blood on the doorpost of your houses. Prepare a special Passover meal. Then get ready to travel."

That night, God's angel killed the oldest boy in every house without the lamb's blood on the doorpost, but passed over those who trusted and followed God's Word. Then Pharaoh told the people of God to go. The people of Egypt gave silver, gold jewelry, and clothes to the Israelites.

God's people left Egypt. God went with them. Then Pharaoh changed his mind. He wanted the Israelites to come back. He and his army chased after them.

The Israelites were now at the shore of the Red Sea. When they saw Pharaoh's army coming, they became afraid. God told Moses to stretch out his hand over the sea, and the waters divided. The people walked across the sea bed on dry ground. Pharaoh and his army tried to follow them. The water came back over them, and they drowned.

God's people praised Him for saving them.

The people of God remembered God's salvation by eating the Passover meal every year at the same time of the year. When the people ate the lamb at this special meal, they remembered how God had saved them and freed them from slavery in Egypt. The Passover lamb also reminds us of the salvation Jesus brought to all people. Just as the blood of the lamb on the doorpost saved God's people in Egypt, the blood Jesus shed on the cross saves all people from their sins.

Blood of the Lamb / Luke 22:15–16

"ah! Mom, I cut my hand," Lindsey screamed. She was peeling potatoes for dinner, and the knife had slipped.

Her mother quickly checked the cut and went to get the antiseptic and the bandages.

"Why won't it quit bleeding?" Lindsey wailed.

"Bleeding helps clean the wound," Mom answered. "Then we use the antiseptic to kill the rest of the germs."

Later, as Lindsey was studying her confirmation lesson about the Passover, she learned how the blood of perfect lambs saved millions of Israelites from death. But it required many lambs to do this.

She remembered also the time that Jesus celebrated the Passover meal with His disciples. They talked of the Old Testament miracle, and then Jesus gave the meal a new, more powerful meaning.

Before the disciples' awe-filled eyes, Jesus proclaimed the bread and wine to be His body and blood, given for the forgiveness of sins. Then He told them to eat this meal "in remembrance" of Him, which we still do today in Holy Communion.

Once again, a perfect Lamb was sacrificed. But this sacrifice required only one Lamb—the perfect Son of God.

Now our just God sees us with Jesus' blood around the door of our heart. We are set free from the slavery of our sins!

Talk about it: You are saved by the blood of the Lamb. Explain. Say a prayer thanking Jesus for sacrificing Himself to save you.

Prayer: Father God, when I think of You sacrificing Your only Son for me, I don't know what to say. Thanks for sending Jesus to be my Savior. Help me to live my life for Him. In the name of Jesus I pray. Amen.

These all look to You, to give them their food in due season. When You give it to them, they gather it up; when You open Your hand, they are filled with good things. Psalm 104:27–28

Manna in the Wilderness | Exodus 15:22–17:6

The people of Israel were happy to leave Egypt, but they were not happy to live in the desert. They didn't trust God to take care of them. Water was hard to find, and they were thirsty. They became angry at Moses. They were even angry at God.

God loved the people and helped them. He gave them water to drink, but then the people were hungry. They wanted meat. They wanted bread. Once again, they became angry at Moses and at God. Once again, God took care of His people. He sent them birds to eat. And He made a special food for them.

God made a bread that the people called manna. It was thin like a cracker, and it had a honey flavor. The people would pick it up off the ground every morning. God told them to take only enough to eat for the day. God fed the people manna each day for forty years! Praise God! Each day, He takes care of our needs too. He gives us forgiveness, food, and so much more.

God's Daily Care / Matthew 6:34

David burst into his classroom just in time. His books and papers were flying, and his shoelaces trailed behind him like mice tails. He scooped his stuff off the floor and scurried to his desk.

"Good morning, David. Please tie your shoes," said Mr. Springer.

David was shuffling through his desk attempting to organize things. Mr. Springer and the rest of the class waited. And waited.

"David. Shoes." Mr. Springer said pointing to David's feet. "I'm glad you're not a centipede; we'd be waiting all day!"

David smiled as he thought about being a centipede. *My parents couldn't afford all those shoes*, he thought. David bent over to tie his *only* pair.

David's family had to be careful with their money. They had medical bills to pay, his brother was in college, and his grandmother lived in their extra bedroom. But David and his family tried not to worry about the future. They knew God would care for them each day.

When we pray the Lord's Prayer, we ask that God will give us our "daily" bread "this day." These words remind us to not be greedy and wasteful, but to live with confidence that God will provide for our needs on a daily basis.

Many stories in the Bible remind us how much God loves and cares for us. Long ago, God took care of His people as they journeyed through the wilderness to the Promised Land. God gave them special food to eat and even made it possible that their clothes did not wear out as they traveled. Jesus once talked about birds and flowers to teach the people about God's care. Birds and flowers don't worry about food or clothing, Jesus noted. We're worth more than they, so surely God will give us every necessity. Clothing, food, house, family, and friends—these earthly treasures all come from God, who loves us because of Jesus.

God also gives us treasures in heaven. These treasures are more valuable than earthly treasures. Jesus bought heavenly treasures for us by His cross and empty tomb. So, even if we don't have much on earth, we're rich! We're taken care of. We have things that really count.

Talk about it: Why are you worth more than animals, birds, or flowers? Name some of the blessings God gives you each day. Use these in a thank-You prayer.

Prayer: Dear Father in heaven, thank You for providing me with both earthly and heavenly treasures, especially faith, forgiveness, and an eternal future with You. Thanks for sending Jesus to make these blessings possible. In His name I pray. Amen.

Love is the fulfilling of the law. Romans 13:10

God Gives the Ten Commandments | Exodus 19–20

The people of Israel walked through the desert. After a while, they came to a mountain called Sinai. This was a very special mountain. God called to Moses from the mountain. He told Moses His plans for the people of Israel. God said, "You are My people. I will do great things for you, and you must obey Me." The people agreed to obey God.

But they needed to know how to obey God. So God told Moses to climb up the mountain. He wanted to give Moses a gift for the people. God gave them the Ten Commandments.

In the Commandments, God told the people not to worship anyone or anything but Him. He told them not to use His name in wrong ways. God wanted the people to have a day of rest and worship each week. He also told them to obey their parents and leaders. He commanded His people not to murder or steal. Husbands and wives should respect each other and their marriage. God told His people not to speak bad things or do bad things. People should not be jealous or try to get others in trouble.

Now the people knew what God expected. It is not easy to obey all these rules. In fact, we can't do it. We need God's help and forgiveness through Jesus, our Savior.

No Rules / 1 Timothy 4:8

"Why do we have to have rules?" Monica moaned, "Why can't we have one day without any rules?"

Mom, who was busy cutting vegetables for dinner, answered, "I don't think you'll be pleased, but if you really want to, we'll give it a try. Saturday will be a no-rules day."

Saturday morning finally arrived, but it didn't go as Monica thought it would. From her bed, she called, "Mom, Kurtis is making too much noise, and I can't sleep."

"Well," Mom said, "remember, there are no rules today."

"You're right," Monica said. She smiled, "As long as I'm up, I guess I'll have ice cream for breakfast. Then I'll watch TV."

But when Monica hopped on the couch in the living room, there was Kurtis, watching his favorite TV show. Monica complained to Mom. But Mom said, "I'm not going to make Kurtis share the TV. Remember, there are no rules today."

Before long, Monica realized that having a no rules day was only making things worse. Eating ice cream and candy for meals was fun, but by the afternoon Monica's stomach ached and she wanted some real food.

"Mom, I thought today was going to be the best day ever, but nothing is turning out right. I'm ready to go back to having rules."

Mom laughed softly and hugged her daughter. "I see you've figured out how important rules can be," she said. "Rules are made because of love, not because someone wants to be mean. Rules help us to live together in peace and fairness."

Just as moms and dads give their children rules, God gives His people the Ten Commandments. The Ten Commandments are also called the Law of God. God arranged the Ten Commandments on tablets of stone and gave them to Moses, but He also wrote the Law on all human hearts. God gave humans the Ten Commandments because He knows what is best for us. But God also knows that obeying these commandments perfectly is completely impossible for humans. That's why He sent Jesus to save us by taking the punishment for our sin.

Talk about it: How can we learn to follow God's will? Which of God's rules is hardest for you to keep?

Prayer: Dear God, thank You for giving me rules. Help me obey them, and forgive me for Jesus' sake when I disobey them. Amen.

Great is the LORD, and greatly to be praised;
He is to be feared above all gods. Psalm 96:4

Aaron Makes an Idol | Exodus 32

Across the Red Sea from Egypt, in the desert wilderness, God miraculously provided for His people. Each day, He placed a thin, light bread called manna on the ground. In addition, God sent flocks of quail for the people to eat. He gave them water to drink, even causing it to pour out of a rock. God wanted His people to know the best and happiest way to live, so at Mount Sinai He gave them the Ten Commandments.

The Commandments were written on two great tablets of stone. While Moses remained on the mountain listening to God, the people grew restless. They didn't know if Moses would return. They complained to Aaron, who was Moses' brother. They asked Aaron to make them a golden statue to worship like the Egyptian people did. Aaron gave in to the people. He told them to give him the gold they had taken from Egypt.

From their gold, Aaron made a calf figure. He built an altar before the calf, and the people began to worship it and celebrate. When Moses approached the camp and saw the golden idol, he threw the two stone tablets containing the Ten Commandments to the ground, breaking them. In anger, Moses ground the golden calf into powder, mixed it with water, and made the people drink it. The people recognized their sin. Moses pleaded with God for the people, and God forgave them. This makes us think of Jesus, who pleads for us and for our forgiveness. Jesus earned forgiveness for all our sins when He died for us on the cross.

Fans of God / Matthew 4:10; 1 John 5:21

Sid loves paintball. He reads paintball magazines. He wears paintball shirts. He spends his time and money on paintball games. Sid is a paintball fanatic. That means he is a fan who thinks of nothing other than paintball.

Do you know anyone like Sid? Do you know anyone who loves a hobby so much that he or she gives little time or attention to anything else? Fanatics can have good goals or interests like getting good grades, being neat, or taking care of a pet. Their goals might include becoming good at computer games or sports or physical fitness.

God has given us a world full of things He wants us to enjoy. Spending time and attention on those things isn't wrong.

However, when our hobbies and interests keep us from focusing on anything or anyone else, we are in danger of worshiping them. We are in danger of loving them more than anything else. We are in danger of loving them even more than God. We are in danger of putting them first in our lives, even before God's will.

God commands us, "You shall have no other gods before Me" (Exodus 20:3). Your "god" is the thing or person you love most. We can tell what or whom we love most by looking at how we spend our time, attention, and money. Since God our heavenly Father gives us everything—including a Savior who loves and forgives us—He desires that we love Him most of all.

How can we be fans of God? We can't do it by ourselves. The Holy Spirit makes us fans of God through God's Word and Sacraments. With His strength and guidance, we have the power to live our lives differently. When we don't put God first in our lives, we sin. And for that sin, we are guilty and need Jesus' forgiveness. The Holy Spirit leads us to live changed lives. He helps us keep paintball, soccer, music, and computer games in perspective—God first; other stuff second.

Talk about it: Can you think of times when you put something that you love before God? When we fail to put God first, we can remember that Jesus forgives us. He leads us to live new lives for Him.

Prayer: Dear God, thank You for filling my world with so many wonderful things. Forgive me when I put other things before You. Through Your Spirit, help me to love and serve You as You desire. Amen.

Be strong and courageous. Do not be frightened, and do not be dismayed, for the LORD your God is with you wherever you go.
Joshua 1:9

Twelve Spies Sent to Canaan | Numbers 13–14

A year after leaving Egypt, the Lord told Moses to send one man from each of the twelve tribes of Israel as a spy to explore the land God had promised to His people. After forty days, the spies returned with a cluster of grapes so huge that two people carried it suspended from a pole. They also brought back pomegranates and figs.

The spies said, "The land surely flows with milk and honey! But the people of the land are strong, and the city is well fortified. We even saw giants there. The people there are stronger than we are." Two of the spies, Joshua and Caleb, didn't agree with the rest. They said, "We need not be afraid of the people, because the Lord is with us." But the people of Israel were afraid. They said, "If only we would have died in Egypt or in the wilderness!" They even talked about choosing another leader and returning to Egypt.

The Lord said to Moses, "Because these people who have seen My glory and the miracles I did in Egypt and in the wilderness have not listened to Me, those twenty years old and older shall not see the land I promised to give them—except for Joshua and Caleb. The people will wander in the wilderness for forty years, one year for each day the spies spent in the Promised Land." And so the people of Israel wandered in the desert. After forty years, the people entered the Promised Land. The oldest among them were Joshua and Caleb. They now entered the Promised Land because of their faith. They trusted in God's grace and saving power.

Faith to Proclaim / Romans 5:19

Many centuries ago, seriously wrong ideas and practices could be found in the Christian churches of Europe. People took Baptism and the Lord's Supper lightly, and there was an emphasis on doing good works to earn salvation, instead of relying on God's mercy. To obtain money to run the church, methods were used that go against what the Bible teaches. One of those methods was the sale of indulgences. Indulgences were papers saying that heaven could be earned by giving money to charity.

Martin Luther was a priest (a worker in the church somewhat like our pastor) and a professor of theology during that time. On October 31, 1517, he posted his Ninety-five Theses on the door of the Castle Church in Wittenberg, Germany. These theses were a series of statements that spoke against the sale of indulgences. Luther believed God's Word, which says that people can be saved only through faith in Jesus Christ. He believed that God's forgiving grace makes us righteous (put right with God).

Luther was eventually excommunicated, or removed, from the Roman Catholic Church by Pope Leo X. He was labeled an outlaw. But Luther believed that Jesus had saved him from his sins.

In 1529, Luther wrote the Small Catechism. A catechism is an instruction book written in the form of questions and answers. Luther's Small Catechism uses the Holy Bible to explain how and why we as Christians use the Ten Commandments, the Apostles' Creed, the Lord's Prayer, Holy Baptism, Confession, and Holy Communion.

Until his death in 1546, Martin Luther continued to proclaim Jesus as the only way to salvation. Like Luther, we are blessed to know that God saves us through Jesus. Because of Jesus' death and resurrection, God has given us the most precious gift. We cannot earn it or pay for it by buying indulgences. Salvation is God's free gift in Jesus Christ, our Lord. We can learn more about God's free gift by studying God's Word and the Small Catechism.

Talk about it: Read Ephesians 2:8. Based on this verse, why do you think Martin Luther disagreed with the selling of indulgences?

Prayer: Dear Jesus, there is nothing in this world that I can do to gain heaven on my own. Thank You for being my Savior and for earning for me the free gift that saves me. Amen.

The Israelites and the Bronze Serpent | Numbers 21:4–9

While the people of Israel wandered in the desert, they were not always happy. They questioned whether they really wanted to be God's people. God made them wander for forty years. During this time, the people often grumbled against God and Moses. They complained about the food God had given them to eat and about the lack of water. God sent poisonous snakes that bit the people, causing many to die.

When the people confessed their sin, Moses pleaded with God to save them. God told Moses to make a snake out of bronze and place it on a pole. Anyone who believed and looked at the bronze snake when bitten was healed and lived. Later, Jesus compared Himself to the bronze snake on the wooden pole, because He knew He would be placed on a wooden cross. Jesus died on the cross so that whoever looked to Him in faith as the Savior would live eternally.

Dare to Be Different / John 15:12–16

Have you ever tried on a pair of wooden shoes? Since before 1300, the people of the Netherlands have worn wooden shoes to protect their feet from the wetness of the land. The shoes insulate their feet, guard them from injury, improve circulation, and give excellent support. The Dutch people dare to be different than the rest of the world. They know the benefits of wooden shoes!

As baptized Christians, we dare to be different because we know the benefits of God's grace. God's grace includes all the good things Jesus earned for us through His life, death, and resurrection.

The world shakes its head in disbelief at our faith in our Lord to give us His grace in water, bread, and wine in the Sacraments. It wonders at us when we explain that God uses a man, our pastor, to share His grace in pronouncing in the Absolution that Jesus has forgiven our sins.

Sometimes, we wonder too. We wonder because all of this Word-and-Sacrament talk seems out of line with the things of the world. We end up acting like the children of Israel wanting more than manna—more than God's grace.

But God uses His Word to remind us, "Be still, and know that I am God. I will be exalted among the nations" (Psalm 46:10). We exalt or lift up God when we honor the places where He is present—His Word and Sacraments. Through these means of God's Word, Baptism, and the Lord's Supper, God provides healing, salvation, and strength to live differently than those in the world around us who are still held captive to sin.

We are different because God is different. We come to church to get away from the world for a brief while and to be with our Lord. He washes our sins away, gives us Himself, and sends us out into the world again to share His love. We can dare to be different because we have the strength God gives us freely in Christ Jesus through God's Word and the Sacraments.

Talk about it: Do you know someone who has dared to be different in God's eyes? Say a prayer of thanksgiving for that person.

 *Prayer: Thank You for Your Word and the Sacraments and for the identity we have through these means to live as Your people. Give me Your courage and the boldness to be different from the world. In Jesus' name I pray. Amen*

God Gives Joshua Victory | The Book of Joshua

After Moses died, God made Joshua the leader of His people. He told Joshua to be bold and courageous, because God was with him. When Joshua led the children of Israel across the Jordan River into the Promised Land, God provided a miracle; He parted the floodwaters so the people crossed over on dry ground. Then God miraculously brought down the walls of Jericho so the army of Israel could easily capture the city.

Joshua and his army conquered the land just as God had promised Moses; and Joshua divided Canaan among the tribes of Israel. After the Lord gave the people rest from war, Joshua called all Israel together and said to them, "I am old and advanced in years; I am going the way of all the earth; and you know that not one thing of all the good things the Lord has spoken concerning you has failed to come to pass. Choose this day whom you will serve. But as for me and my house, we will serve the Lord."

And the people answered, "We also will serve the Lord; for He is God."

The Toughest Foe / Deuteronomy 31:7–8

Marcy loves to play basketball. As a college athlete, she set scoring and rebounding records. She had planned to graduate and then teach math in a high school.

All these plans were put on hold when Marcy got a phone call from her doctor a few days after graduation. She had Hodgkin's disease, a type of cancer. On the basketball court, she had faced many opponents and won. Now she told her mother, "This is my toughest foe yet."

Trusting in God's love and care for her, Marcy moved confidently ahead with the treatments. She experienced pain, discomfort, and plenty of needles. But the treatments helped. Eventually, the cancer was defeated and Marcy began to realize her dream of teaching in a high school.

What is your toughest foe? Is it living peaceably with your brother or sister? putting up with the bully at school? trying to find peace in a family that seems to be breaking apart? telling your friend about Jesus? Or is it a dreaded illness, like cancer?

Joshua could have been overwhelmed with fear. He was taking over leadership of the unruly Israelites. They wouldn't obey Moses. Why would they obey him? Joshua's task was also enormous. He was to chase out the Canaanites so Israel could take over the land promised long ago to Abraham and his descendants. There were many walled cities and strong enemies to conquer.

But Moses reminded Joshua, "The Lord Himself goes before you and will be with you." We have that promise too, no matter how tough our foes. Through faith, given by the Holy Spirit, Jesus lives in us, forgives our sins, and strengthens us to face every foe.

Talk about it: Why would Joshua feel frightened? How can we get help to face our toughest foes?

Prayer: Dear Father, give us Your courage and strength to face every foe. Help us remember that You will always be with us. Amen.

Fear not, for I have redeemed you; I have called you by name, you are Mine. Isaiah 43:1

Gideon | Judges 6–7

God brought His people into the land He had promised to give them. Later, the people were unfaithful to God and did evil things. Then, some enemies fought God's people. God allowed the enemies to win. At last, the people remembered to pray to the Lord to save them.

God called Gideon to lead His people against the enemy. Gideon was afraid. He didn't want to be the leader. But God promised to be with him and help him. Many people came together to fight the enemy. God told Gideon, "You have too many

people. They will trust their own power. They need to put their trust in Me." Gideon told the soldiers, "If you don't want to be soldiers anymore, go home."

Many left. God told Gideon, "You still have too many." Gideon took the men to the water for a drink. Three hundred men drank water by putting it to their mouth in their hands. God chose them to be His soldiers. They had unusual weapons: a trumpet in one hand and a torch inside a clay pitcher in their other hand. At night, they surrounded the enemy in the valley below. Then they blew their trumpets, broke the pitchers, and held the torches in the air. The enemy soldiers were so confused that they started to kill one another. God delivered His people from their enemies.

When we become afraid, we can trust in God to be with us. God is always with us. He will help us.

Earthshaking / Haggai 2:6–7

Have you ever heard the term *earthshaking*? What could be so powerful that it could make the earth shake? When your teacher surprises you with a science test, it might not be earthshaking, even if your knees wobble.

The music you play could be powerful enough to shake the house. So could your dad's voice when he asks you to turn it down.

Stampeding horses can cause the earth to shake. Stampeding children on their way to the refrigerator after school probably could too.

The powerful force of hurricane winds can shake trees and do immense damage to homes, churches, and other buildings. People who live in parts of the world hit by earthquakes have seen the destructive power of the earth as its layers shift.

History has shown that an atomic bomb can not only shake but also destroy everything for miles. Could there be anything more powerful than that?

Yes. The power of God. God is powerful enough to shake the heavens and the earth. He is powerful enough to create our world and each of us in it. His love for us is powerful enough to move God to send His Son, Jesus, to die and rise in triumph so that our sins are forgiven.

The God of all power has chosen you to be His child. He sent His Son to defeat our greatest enemies—sin, death, and the devil. He gives you the power to face the things that may cause you to be afraid.

Our powerful God loves you—now *that's* earthshaking news!

Talk about it: What things are you most afraid of? Why do you not need to fear them? How can you share the news of God and His power with others?

Prayer: God of power, God of love, thank You for loving me and making me Your child. Thank You for forgiving my sins for Jesus' sake. Amen.

You are a chosen race, a royal priesthood, a holy nation, a people for His own possession, that you may proclaim the excellencies of Him who called you out of darkness into His marvelous light. 1 Peter 2:9

Samson | Judges 13–16

Manoah and his wife wanted to have a baby. God planned to give them a son. Their son would fight the enemies of God's people. God would use him to fight an enemy called the Philistines. Manoah and his wife named their son Samson. God wanted Samson to let his hair grow long as a sign that he served God. Samson promised never to cut his hair.

God made Samson very strong. One day, a lion attacked Samson. He killed the lion with his bare hands! Samson did many other brave things, using his great strength. He often fought against the Philistines.

The Philistines wanted to know why Samson was so strong. One day, they found out. Samson told his secret to an evil woman named Delilah. The woman cut his hair. Samson had been unfaithful in serving God. Now Samson was weak. The Philistines took him to jail. They poked out his eyes!

The Philistines had a party. They were proud that they had Samson in jail. They thought they were stronger than God's strong man. They chained Samson to a post that held up the building. They made fun of him. But Samson had a surprise for them. Samson remembered the Lord. He prayed that God would make him strong again, and God did. Samson pulled down the building! He killed more than three thousand of God's enemies. But Samson died too.

God gave Samson amazing abilities. His great strength came from God. God gives each of us amazing strengths and abilities too. We can use these things to serve Him.

God used Samson to save His people from the Philistines. God sent Jesus to save us from even greater enemies. Jesus saved us from sin, death, and Satan's power.

Special and Unique / Isaiah 40:29

"Chris, you don't even need a new winter coat," said Mrs. Alexander, trying to stay calm. "Why would you ask for such an expensive one?"

"Mom, all the kids at school have coats like this. I don't want to be different." Chris was almost in tears. When he calmed down, his mother was able to convince him that the coat he had was fine.

Why do some people want to dress or act the way others do? One reason is the need to be accepted or to fit in. Chris thinks if he has a coat like the others, they might include him in more of their activities.

If you sometimes feel this way, remember that God created each of us to be different. He loves us so much that He gave each of us a unique body, smile, personality, and brain. Do you think He wants us to try to be just like everybody else?

Many people in the Bible were "different." Young David stepped out of the crowd of cowards and confronted the giant Goliath. Samuel once lifted a heavy city gate to the top of a hill. John the Baptist was unconventional. He wore animal skins and ate bugs!

Each of these people accepted themselves as God had created them. They used their God-given talents to glorify the name of the Lord.

God created us individually, and He loves each of us personally. Jesus came to rescue every lost person who has strayed from God, including each of us.

Through the power of His Spirit, we can be what God wants us to be. And we can serve Him with the unique talents and abilities He has given to us.

Talk about it: How might you help Chris realize it isn't important to be like everyone else? Why is it important to do the best you can with what God has given you?

Prayer: Dear Lord, what a magnificent God You are! You made each of us special. Help me discover my talents and use them to glorify Your name. For the sake of Jesus I ask it. Amen.

I praise You, for I am fearfully
and wonderfully made.
Wonderful are Your works;
my soul knows it very well.
Psalm 139:14

Hannah and Samuel | 1 Samuel 1:1–2:26

Children were important to the people of Israel, just as they are important to people today. Hannah and Elkanah wanted to have a baby. Hannah prayed for children. She made a promise to God. Hannah said, "If God will give me a child, I will give the child back to Him." She meant that her child would live at the tabernacle, the tent church. He would serve God.

One day while she prayed, a priest named Eli was watching her. Hannah was praying from her heart. Her lips were moving, but she was not speaking. Eli thought she had drunk too much wine! He told her to go home. But Hannah explained that she was praying. Eli said, "Go in peace, and may the God of Israel grant you what you have asked of Him."

God blessed Hannah. She and Elkanah had a son. His name was Samuel. Hannah raised Samuel while he was a baby. When he got older, she kept her promise to God. She took Samuel to serve God. Samuel lived in a room at the tent-church. Once each year, his parents visited him and brought a new robe for him to wear.

Samuel grew up serving God. He had many jobs to do at the tabernacle. God was helping Samuel to grow in faith. God would make Samuel a great leader. In Christ, God leads us to grow in faith and to serve Him with our lives too.

Formed and Knit / Psalm 139:13

If you could change anything about the way you look, would you do it? If you asked your friends this question, you would probably get a loud *yes*. Each day, hundreds of thousands of dollars are spent by people trying to change the shape of their nose, the size of their hips, or other body features.

A little girl once stood in front of a mirror, looking into her deep brown eyes. She shut her eyes tightly and prayed in faith that God would please, please, please make her eyes blue. She opened her eyes, and to her amazement they were still brown! She could not understand why God did not answer her prayer.

That little girl grew up to reach many people for Christ as a missionary in India. She later said that if God had answered her prayer and given her blue eyes, she would not have been as well accepted into the culture of India nor had such a ministry for the Lord among the people who lived where brown eyes are the norm. God's design was best for her work.

The consequences of living in a sin-filled world touch every part of life—even at the very beginning of life. Sometimes, people are born with physical challenges. Does this mean that God made a mistake? No. God is perfect and all-knowing.

Does God love some people more than others? No. God loves all people. Does God have a plan to work all things in our life for His good purpose? Yes. God can use freckles or a wheelchair for good in ways we can't imagine.

Accepting our physical features is acknowledging that God is God. Just as He designed a perfect way of salvation and forgiveness of our sins through Jesus' death and resurrection, He continues working his design in us. We are His workmanship!

Talk about it: What are your unique characteristics?

Prayer: Dear Lord Jesus, thank You for the way You made me. Please help me see Your plan for my life and to serve You in the ways You have planned. In Jesus' name I pray. Amen.

Love covers a multitude of sins.
1 Peter 4:8

David and Jonathan | 1 Samuel 18–20

David was a close friend of Jonathan, a son of King Saul. After God used David to defeat an enemy of the people, women sang a song praising David. They sang, "Saul has killed his thousands and David his ten thousands." Saul became angry and jealous of David's popularity.

When Saul told Jonathan and the servants that they should kill David, Jonathan spoke up on David's behalf. Saul listened to Jonathan and agreed that he would not kill David.

But Saul did not remain true to his word. Soon, Jonathan realized that Saul was again planning to kill David.

Jonathan met with David and told him, "Let me talk to my father again to see what his plans are toward you. In three days, I will come to the place where you are hiding. I will shoot three arrows as if at a target. I will send a boy to find the arrows. If I say to the boy, 'The arrows are on this side of you,' you can come home, for all will be safe. If I say, 'The arrows are farther out,' then you will need to go far away, for all is not well."

Jonathan went out into the field with a boy and shot an arrow. Jonathan said to the boy, "Isn't the arrow farther out? Hurry." When the boy had found the arrows, Jonathan sent him back to the city. When the boy left, David came out of hiding. The two friends wept as they told each other good-bye. Then David left.

What Does It Mean To Be Trustworthy? / Proverbs 11:13

Proverbs 11:13 talks about a sin called gossip. To gossip is to tell someone something bad about another person—something that doesn't need to be told. To be trustworthy, on the other hand, is to keep the bad information quiet; in other words, not speak it to anyone else. The commandment "You shall not give false testimony against your neighbor" tells us that we should not lie to or about other people, hurt anyone's reputation, or betray friends or family. Instead, God commands us to defend and speak well of others.

Sometimes, we defend others when we simply keep quiet about something we know. For example, at a birthday party, Ellie had just gotten back to her seat with a piece of birthday cake when she accidentally tipped her plate sideways and the cake slid off her plate and onto the floor. It was a funny sight, but only Ellie's friend Mandy saw it happen. Rather than laughing loudly and further embarrassing Ellie by drawing attention to what had happened, Mandy quietly helped Ellie clean the cake up off the floor and then encouraged her to simply go and get another piece. Mandy showed herself to be a good friend to Ellie.

Jesus is the same kind of friend to us. Rather than allowing us to experience the consequences of our own misbehaviors, Jesus stepped in and helped us by cleaning up our mess. He died for our sins and then spoke up for us before His Father in heaven. Jesus declares us not guilty of our sins because He has taken them all away.

By His love, He gives us the desire to also show we are good friends to others by speaking well of them and sometimes by remaining silent as a way of being a good friend to others.

Talk about it: Why do you think telling and hearing gossip is so tempting? Has anyone ever gossiped about you? How did it make you feel?

Prayer: Dear Lord Jesus, thank You for saving me. Forgive me for the times I have used words to say things that have been unkind and hurtful. Please help me to speak up in defense of others, especially for those who are in need. Help me always to speak in a trustworthy way. I pray in Your name. Amen.

If we say we have no sin, we deceive ourselves, and the truth is not in us. If we confess our sins, He is faithful and just to forgive us our sins and to cleanse us from all unrighteousness. 1 John 1:8–9

David Repents | 2 Samuel 11–12

According to God's plan, David became the king of Israel after Saul. One spring, instead of going out to battle with his troops, David remained in Jerusalem, the capital city. As David walked on the roof of the palace one night, he saw Bathsheba, the wife of a soldier named Uriah. David saw that Bathsheba was very beautiful, so he sent for her. Later, when Bathsheba sent word to David saying she was pregnant with his child, David wrote a letter to Joab, the commander of the army. David asked to arrange for Uriah to be killed in battle. After Joab did as David asked, David took Bathsheba to be his wife, but these events displeased the Lord.

The Lord sent the prophet Nathan to David. Nathan said, "There were two men in a city, one rich and the other poor. The rich man had many flocks and herds, but the poor man had only one lamb, which he loved as though it were his child.

When a guest came to visit the rich man, instead of taking a lamb from his own flocks, he took the poor man's lamb and killed it and cooked it for the traveler to eat." When David heard this story, he became angry and said, "As surely as the Lord lives, the man who did this thing deserves to die."

Nathan said to David, "You are that man. You have taken Uriah's wife to be your wife after you killed him with the sword of your enemies."

David then realized his sinfulness. "I have sinned against the Lord," he confessed.

Nathan said, "The Lord has put away your sin. You will not die. But the child that will be born to you and Bathsheba will die." Then Nathan left. The child born to Bathsheba became very sick and died. Later, Bathsheba and David had another son. They named him Solomon, and the Lord loved him.

Peace through Forgiveness / Colossians 1:19–23

I hate you!" Heather screamed. "I never want to talk to you again." She ran into her room and slammed the door.

"That's just fine with me!" Joel yelled back, slamming his bedroom door twice as hard.

It's hard being a brother or a sister. Living so close in the family offers lots of opportunities for hurt feelings, dinged pride, and outright anger. That closeness gives Satan many opportunities to tempt, and it offers us many opportunities to sin. And sin always separates. It leads to two people sitting alone in separate rooms.

Joel wondered what he should do. He had been pretty hard on Heather. The teasing went too far this time. He was sorry, but what could he do? In the past, he had gone to Heather and said, "I'm sorry." She usually said, "Forget it." But that didn't seem to settle the issue. There was still hurt and remembered anger.

Perhaps Joel could take a clue from God. Every time we separate ourselves from Him by some sin, He is willing to forgive. When in sorrow over the sin we come back to God and ask for forgiveness, He lovingly takes us back. Because of Jesus' death on the cross, He brings us together with Himself again. He doesn't allow the sin to stand between us and Him.

Joel tried the Christian way. He knocked on Heather's door. An angry "Go away!" was her response.

"Heather, I was wrong to say the things I said. I'm sorry." Joel said. "Please forgive me. I've asked God to, and now I'm asking you."

Heather opened the door a crack, then all the way. Tearfully, but with a smile, she said, "I forgive you, Joel. Please forgive me too for the things I said."

The separation was over. Sin had been confessed. Forgiveness had been asked for and received. Joel and Heather now knew peace through the cross of Jesus, their Lord.

Talk about it: Think about a disagreement you have had with a friend, family member, or even an enemy. How did you handle it? Is there still separation between you and that person? Is it time to say, "I'm sorry; please forgive me"?

Prayer: Father, I cause so much separation because of my sin. I don't want to be separated from You. In Jesus' name, forgive me. Please heal any separation between me and anyone else. Help me to ask for forgiveness. And when others ask for my forgiveness, help me give it as freely and eagerly as You forgive me. Amen.

Desire when it has conceived gives birth to sin, and sin when it is fully grown brings forth death. James 1:15

David and Absalom | 2 Samuel 14–19

David's son Absalom was admired because he was handsome and had a beautiful head of hair. When Absalom traveled, he made an impressive sight, with chariots, horses, and fifty running men. Absalom liked to greet people as they came to see the king. He made himself popular by saying they would have justice if he were king. But his words were lies. Absalom did not speak out of concern for the people, but rather because he wanted to turn the hearts of the people away from King David.

Absalom went to Hebron and sent spies throughout all of Israel. The spies said, "When you hear the sound of the trumpet, say, 'Absalom is king in Hebron.'" The conspiracy became strong as Absalom's popularity among the people rose.

A messenger came to King David saying, "The hearts of the men of Israel are with Absalom." So David and his family and servants fled from the capital city of Jerusalem. David crossed the brook Kidron and went up the Mount of Olives, weeping as he went, barefoot and with his head covered. Meanwhile, Absalom came into Jerusalem.

David organized those who were with him, making some men captains over the rest. He commanded, "Deal gently with Absalom." David's army went to battle against the army of Absalom. David's army was victorious. Absalom was trying to escape from David's men when his mule went under the thick branches of a great oak tree. Absalom's head got caught in the oak, suspending him in the air.

When David's commander, Joab, learned of this, he took three javelins and plunged them into Absalom's heart, killing him. Then Joab blew the trumpet to end the battle. When David heard that Absalom was dead, he wept and said, "O my son Absalom! If only I had died instead of you."

The Truth Matters / John 14:6

Once, a man was speeding down a winding road. Seemingly out of nowhere, a man on a bike appeared. The speeding driver swerved and slammed on his brakes, but he was too late. He hit the man on the bike. The bicyclist was badly hurt, but the driver was afraid to take him to the hospital or call 911 for fear of getting in trouble. Instead, he drove away from the scene of the accident. Not long afterward, a semitrailer rounded the corner and, unable to stop in time, hit the bicyclist again, injuring him even more seriously. But this driver called for help.

Reports about the first driver who did not help the injured cyclist filled every news station, but that did not make him come forward and confess. He read articles on the front page of the newspaper, but that did not make the sinful man confess either. He denied his guilt.

You see, already years earlier, this man had begun a pattern of sin. His father owned a special watch and forbade anyone from touching it. But one day, as a boy, this man played with the watch and accidentally broke it. To cover up his sin, he put the pieces back in his father's drawer and denied that he had done it. He lied.

This lie led to more lies. The boy who lied became the man who lied. He lied so much that he often convinced himself that the lie was actually the truth.

Satan is called the "father of lies." He tempts us into believing that the truth doesn't matter. More than that, he works tirelessly to bring us into hell. Every single one of us is sinful, just like the man in the story. We lie and believe that it's okay. After all, who wants to get in trouble? But liars are sinful, and liars need a Savior.

Jesus is the Son of God. As John 14:6 says, He is "the way, and the truth, and the life." The only way to be saved from sin, death, and the devil is through Him! He is life—eternal life. Jesus is the Savior God sent for you and for me and for the man who lied. And guess what? Jesus never lies. We can rejoice in the knowledge that our sins are wiped clean and that one day we will live in heaven with the Lord.

Forgiveness and eternal life can be found only in Jesus Christ. And though the devil may try to convince us otherwise, any promise of salvation outside of faith in Jesus is a lie. As followers of Jesus, we know that the truth matters.

Talk about it: Read 1 John 5:11–12. What is the good news offered in these verses? What does this good news mean to us as Christians?

 *Prayer: Dear Lord, You are truth. Thank You for dying on Calvary for me so that I might be free from the power of sin. Help me to always remember that You are the only way to truth and eternal life. In Your name I pray. Amen.*

Solomon Builds a Temple | 1 Kings 5–8

King David loved the one true God. He wanted to build a temple for God. But God wanted Solomon to build the temple. Solomon was David's son. David made plans for the temple. He asked the people to give money and other things for the temple. The people gave gladly. Now his son Solomon could build the temple. Like David, Solomon loved and served the one true God. He wanted to build a beautiful house for God.

King Solomon paid workers to build the temple. He bought the best wood, stone, and gold. Workers used the stone to build high walls.

Inside, they used beautiful wood. They wanted God's house of worship to be very special. It took seven years to build the temple. They built a room called the Most Holy Place. They hung a beautiful curtain across the entrance to the Most Holy Place. Behind the curtain, they placed the ark of the covenant—the golden box that held the Ten Commandments. Only the high priest could enter the Most Holy Place. It was a special place for the only true God. God showed He was happy with the temple. He came in a bright cloud that filled the rooms. Solomon and the people prayed. The people praised God for fourteen days!

The One True God / Psalm 31:14

Do you like optical illusions, such as the picture that looks like two heads facing each other, but then looks like a vase? Or how about the illusion where one line looks longer than the other, but they are really the same length? Then there is that one with the steps—are they going up or down?

Different people can most certainly see the same thing different ways. Different ways of looking at things can be fun when looking at optical illusions, but when speaking about our faith, different views can be a matter of life or death.

In our society, the word *god* has become very popular. We hear government officers, movie stars, and people in our communities speak about a god. You may hear your friends talk about god.

Are you wondering why the word *god* isn't capitalized here? It's not a mistake. It's not an optical illusion. It is not capitalized because many people use the word *god,* yet they are not talking about God. They are not speaking of the true, triune God—Father, Son, and Holy Spirit—the God who sent His only Son to die for us.

Just because people talk about god doesn't mean they believe in Jesus. They may be thinking about things very differently than you. Ask them what they mean. Ask them why they believe and worship their god. Ask them if they can be sure they are going to heaven. If their answers don't include Jesus, then the Holy Spirit might use you to lead them to faith in the only true God.

Talk about it: The only true God is the triune God—Father, Son, and Holy Spirit. Talk about the difference between the generic god and the triune God.

Prayer: Dear Father, Son, and Holy Spirit, You alone can save from sin and death. Use me to invite others to hear Your message proclaimed and taught so that they may believe Your love for them. Amen.

Elijah Defeats the Prophets of Baal | 1 Kings 18

After the reign of Solomon, the kingdom of Israel divided into two parts, and many of the people began to worship idols. They called one of the idols Baal. During the third year of a famine, God's prophet Elijah spoke before the people gathered at Mount Carmel. He said, "How long will you waver between two opinions? If the Lord is God, follow Him. If Baal, then follow him. I am the only prophet of the Lord; yet there are 450 prophets of Baal. Give us two bulls. Let the prophets of Baal lay one bull on the wood of their altar, but place no fire under it. I will lay the other on the wood of the altar to God and place no fire under it. Call on the name of your gods, and I will call on the name of the Lord; and the God that sends fire, let Him be recognized as the true God." The people agreed.

From morning until noon the prophets of Baal called for their idol to send fire. During the afternoon, they cut themselves until blood flowed, in hopes of gaining Baal's favor and attention.

Elijah took twelve stones (the same number as the tribes of Israel) and built an altar to God. Around the altar, he dug a trench. Then he laid the bull on the wood of the altar and drenched the sacrifice, the wood, and the altar with water until it filled the trenches. Elijah called on the name of the Lord: "Let it be known today that You are God in Israel and that I am Your servant. Hear me, O Lord, that these people may know that You are the Lord God and that You have turned their hearts back again."

Suddenly, fire from the Lord consumed the sacrifice, the wood, the stones, the dust, and even the water that was in the trench. When the people saw what had happened, they said, "The LORD, He is God; the LORD, He is God." With these words, the people honored God's name. They praised God for His great and awesome goodness.

God's Name / Psalm 103:1

Ann rushed up to her teacher, Mrs. Lerner, and gave her a hug. Mrs. Lerner had just been given a plaque for being a teacher for twenty-five years.

"Can I look at your plaque?" asked Ann. Mrs. Lerner smiled and handed Ann the shiny plaque. Ann noticed words carved into the metal that said, "To God Be Glory."

"To God Be Glory?" Ann was confused. "But Mrs. Lerner, you're the one doing all the work."

Mrs. Lerner put her hands on Ann's shoulders and smiled, "I live every single day in God's grace—in His love," she said. "I always want to glorify God with my gifts, and I never want to teach or say anything about God that could be wrong or misleading. That's what that phrase means."

Mrs. Lerner gave Ann a good answer. God gave her the ability to teach, and she wouldn't be able to succeed without God's help. By striving to teach God's Word faithfully and purely, Mrs. Lerner kept God's name holy.

Sometimes, our sinfulness gets in the way of us giving God the glory. We sin. We do things that God forbids us to do. We may even lead others away from God with our words and actions.

That's why in the Lord's Prayer we pray, "Hallowed be Thy name." To hallow is to honor as holy. God's name is holy because He is holy. When we sin, we profane His name. We pray instead that God would help us lead holy lives. When we live holy lives, we honor and keep God's name holy.

Thank God for the forgiveness we have in Jesus. Thank God also for parents, teachers, and others who help us learn about Him.

Talk about it: What are some ways to honor God's name?

Prayer: Dear Jesus, in Baptism, You gave me Your name as I was baptized in the name of the Father and of the Son and of the Holy Spirit. Thank You for washing away my sins and for working in me so that I might glorify You in all I do and say. Help me to keep Your name holy. Amen.

[Jesus] said to them, "Take care, and be on your guard against all covetousness, for one's life does not consist in the abundance of his possessions." Luke 12:15

Ahab Steals Naboth's Vineyard | 1 Kings 21–22

After Solomon's time, there reigned over Israel a wicked king named Ahab. Ahab wanted a vineyard that belonged to a man named Naboth. He wanted it so much that he sinned. The sin of wanting something in a wrong way is called coveting. Ahab coveted Naboth's vineyard. When Naboth refused to sell it to him, Ahab went to bed upset. He pouted and refused to get up and eat. His wicked wife, Jezebel, came to him and said, "Get up and eat and be happy; I will get the vineyard for you."

Jezebel wrote letters in Ahab's name, sealed them with his seal, and sent the letters to the elders and nobles in Naboth's city. She wrote, "Find two men to accuse Naboth of speaking against God and against the king. Then take Naboth out and stone him." After the men did as Jezebel asked, she said to Ahab, "Go and take possession of the vineyard, for Naboth is dead."

God told the prophet Elijah, "Go and meet Ahab in the vineyard of Naboth and tell him that because he has killed Naboth, dogs will lick up his blood in the same place as they licked the blood of Naboth, and dogs shall eat Jezebel by the wall of Jezreel."

Three years later, Ahab was struck with an arrow in battle and blood ran out of the wound into the chariot. So Ahab died. Later, when they washed out the chariot, dogs came and licked up Ahab's blood as God had foretold. God's words about Jezebel came true as well.

The story of King Ahab and Naboth's vineyard shows how the sin of coveting can lead to still other sins. But Jesus died to pay for all sins, including sins involving coveting.

"Gotta Haves" / 1 Timothy 6:6–8

Gotta Haves" pop up all over. Here are some things you might hear them saying:

"But, Mom, everybody's got one—I gotta have it!"

"I've just gotta have those jeans!"

"I don't care how much it costs: I've gotta have it!"

Read 1 Kings 21:1–4. King Ahab was a Gotta Have. When Naboth refused to sell him his vineyard, Ahab sulked and became angry. He refused to eat. (Gotta Haves often act like that.) God called Ahab one of the most evil of all the kings of Israel. His selfishness was part of the evil.

Gotta Haves like King Ahab make life miserable for those around them. They're selfish, and they don't care who knows it. The funny thing is, they're not really all that happy. You see, Gotta Haves are never satisfied. What they gotta have today is not good enough tomorrow. They have always gotta have more.

What's the Christian's attitude toward the things of this life? St. Paul sums it up like this: "I have learned in whatever situation I am to be content" (Philippians 4:11). Then Paul adds this promise: "My God will supply every need of yours according to His riches in glory in Christ Jesus" (4:19).

As tempting as the joys and pleasures of this world may be, only our joy in the Lord and His forgiving love will always be with us and last forever.

Talk about it: What is God's advice to Gotta Haves? What alone brings us true happiness? (Read Habakkuk 3:18.) Why does this make us happy?

Prayer: Dear Lord, forgive me when I am selfish. You are my Savior, and You give me all I need. You lived, died, and rose again to earn forgiveness for all sins, including sins of coveting. For this I thank and praise You. Amen.

Elisha Heals Naaman | 2 Kings 5

Naaman, captain of the army of the king of Syria, had a disease called leprosy. In his household lived a young slave, a girl taken prisoner from the people of Israel. She told Naaman's wife about the prophet in her homeland who could pray to God to cure Naaman of his leprosy. And so Naaman went to see Elisha.

When Naaman arrived, Elisha sent a messenger to tell him to go wash in the Jordan River seven times and he would be healed. Naaman grew angry at Elisha's request. "Aren't the rivers of my homeland better rivers than these?" he raged. Naaman's servants encouraged him to do as the prophet had said.

Naaman listened. He washed seven times in the Jordan, and his leprosy left him. Returning to thank Elisha, Naaman said, "Now I know that there is no God in all the earth except in Israel."

Naaman's washing in the Jordan River reminds us of our Baptism. By faith in Baptism, Jesus washes away our sins, healing us of the sickness of our sins. Water connected with God's Word works wondrous things!

A Special Celebration / Titus 3:5

When Rob woke up, he knew it was a special day. His parents always remembered his Baptism birthday.

Right away, he noticed two things in the kitchen. His Baptism candle stood in the middle of the table with a note: "Happy Baptism Birthday, Rob!" And there was a package next to his plate. When he took off the white bow and wrapping paper, he found a special plaque with his name on it.

At dinner that evening, Rob's Baptism candle was burning. After dinner, Rob's dad led the family in their special Baptism birthday prayer:

"Dear God, thank You for washing each of us clean in Baptism. Remind us that You have forgiven all our sins because of what Your Son, Jesus, did for us on the cross. Let us

wake up each day to live the new life You have given us in our Baptism. Amen."

Then, as Dad gave the blessing, each member of the family made the sign of the cross. "The grace of the Lord Jesus Christ and the love of God and the fellowship of the Holy Spirit be with [us] all. [Amen]" (2 Corinthians 13:14).

Not everyone celebrates their Baptism birthdays like Rob's family, nor does everyone receive gifts like a plaque. However, everyone who is baptized receives treasures much more valuable than earthly gifts and celebrations. All who are baptized receive forgiveness for their sins, protection from death and Satan, and the precious gift of eternal life.

We don't even have to wait for our Baptism birthday to think about how special it is to be a child of God through Baptism.

~~~~~~~~~~~~~~~~~~~~

Talk about it: Talk about ways you can celebrate your Baptism birthday. What are ways you can celebrate your Baptism every day?

Prayer: Dear God, thank You for the precious treasures You have given us through Baptism. Help us to never forget how blessed we are to be Your children. Amen.

Bless the LORD, O my soul, and forget not all His benefits,
who forgives all your iniquity, who heals all your diseases.
Psalm 103:2–3

King Hezekiah Prays and Is Healed | 2 Kings 20:1–11

Old Testament ruler King Hezekiah was sick and about to die. Hezekiah prayed to the Lord, asking God to make him well again. God heard Hezekiah's prayer. God told Hezekiah that He would add fifteen years to Hezekiah's life. Furthermore, God promised Hezekiah that He would deliver him from his enemies, the Assyrians. God promised Hezekiah that He would give him a sign that His promises would come to pass. As a sign, God made the sun go back ten steps on the marker that traced the journey of the sun each day.

God hears and answers all prayers. Sometimes, God says yes. Sometimes, God says no. At other times, God wants us to wait. But God wants us to pray for ourselves and for others, including the members of our family. He wants us to pray that His will be done. He wants us to trust that He knows what is best for us and that He will help us. All help comes from God. God's Word assures us of His love and care. Romans 8:31–32 reminds us "If God is for us, who can be against us? He who did not spare His own Son but gave Him up for us all, how will He not also with Him graciously give us all things?"

God's Will / Isaiah 38:1–8, 16

Samantha looked at her friend Dominique through teary eyelashes. "I'm so sick of hospital gowns, needles, and mushed-up food," she said. "But most of all, I'm just sick of feeling sick."

Dominique didn't know what to say. "I'm praying for you, Sam," she mumbled. "I hope you feel better real soon."

Samantha replied with a tiny smile, "I hope so too!"

Samantha had a great desire to get well. In our Bible reading, King Hezekiah also desired to get well. God had told him through the prophet Isaiah that he would soon die. Hezekiah wept bitterly and pleaded with God to spare His life.

God heard Hezekiah's prayer and promised to add fifteen years to the king's life. God gave Hezekiah a sign—something he could see—to help him believe God's promise. The shadow cast by the sun went back ten steps. Hezekiah got better. God kept His promise!

Many of us have family and friends who face sickness and death. God hates the diseases and sins we battle. He wants us to be well and happy. But even more important, He wants us to have faith in Him so that we will live with Him forever in heaven.

That's why He sent His Son into this world to live and die for us.

As we confess our sins, we remember God's eternal promise to forgive us for Jesus' sake. The power of our Lord's forgiveness restores our broken bodies, our broken spirits, and our broken lives. His will is to make us whole again, preparing us to live eternally in heaven.

Talk about it: Do you know someone who suffers with a long-term sickness? How can you share the message of God's love with that person?

Prayer: Thank You, Lord, for eternally mending my life for the sake of Jesus. Help me live according to Your will. Help me always to trust in You. In Jesus' name I pray. Amen.

For to us a child is born, to us a son is given; and the government shall be upon His shoulder, and His name shall be called Wonderful Counselor, Mighty God, Everlasting Father, Prince of Peace. Isaiah 9:6

Isaiah Tells of Our Savior | Isaiah 9; 53

Shortly after God first gave His people the Ten Commandments, they worshiped a god they had made for themselves in the form of a golden calf. But then the people repented of their sin, and God forgave them. Through the years, however, God's people often fell into the sin of idolatry. Then God sent special messengers called prophets to call them to repentance.

One of these prophets was Isaiah. He lived some seven hundred years before Jesus' birth. Still, by the power of God's Spirit, Isaiah wrote about Jesus—the Savior who would come to earn forgiveness for all sins, including the sin of idolatry. Isaiah described Jesus, writing about the very names by which Jesus would be called. These different names for Jesus tell us about Him.

Here are a few:

Wonderful Counselor. A counselor listens patiently and advises wisely (Isaiah 9:6).

Mighty God. The word *mighty* speaks of His power as true God (Isaiah 9:6).

Everlasting Father. A father protects his children, provides for them, and cares deeply about them. Everlasting means "never ending" (Isaiah 9:6).

Prince of Peace. A peaceful ruler brings contentment and well-being to his people (Isaiah 9:6).

Immanuel. It means "God with us" (Isaiah 7:14).

These names for Jesus tell us that He is a powerful God who protects us, cares for us, and listens patiently to us. He came from heaven to make us His own and to win salvation for us. He is a peaceful ruler who is and always will be with us. And best of all, He is God's Son, our Savior.

"O God!" / Exodus 20:7

One spring, Nico went to stay with his grandmother in the country. She took him to the grocery store in her new car to pick out some of his favorite foods. On the way home, Grandma suddenly became very ill and was unable to control the car. Nico took hold of the steering wheel. "O God!" he said.

He unfastened his seat belt and reached over to move his grandmother's foot off the gas pedal. As the car slowed down he concentrated on steering to the side of the road. He managed to get his foot on the brake. At first, he pushed a little too hard, but he got the car stopped. He phoned 911 and his parents, and an ambulance quickly came and took Grandma and Nico to the hospital.

Nico's story was on the news, and he was called a hero. The reporter asked him what made him so brave. Nico gave the honor to God. He said, "God helped me."

Remember the part in the story when Nico said, "O God!"? Sometimes people use God's name for no reason at all. Speaking God's name carelessly breaks the Second Commandment and is forbidden by God. But when Nico called out God's name, it was a prayer for help. In Psalm 50:15, God says, "Call upon Me in the day of trouble; I will deliver you, and you shall glorify Me."

God loves us very much. He knows when we need help. After all, He sent Jesus to help us with our greatest problem—sin. We shouldn't say God's name carelessly, but just like Nico, we can call on God's name when we are in need. We know for sure that He will help us.

Talk about it: In our society, we hear God's name being misused a lot. We hear His name being used carelessly on television, in movies, and maybe even from classmates, friends, or family members. Why do you suppose this is? How can you set a good example for others when it comes to using God's name correctly?

Prayer: Thank You, God, for giving us Your name to call upon in times of trouble. Help me to remember to give Your name glory and respect, and forgive me when I mess up. In Jesus' holy name I pray. Amen.

God Saves the Three Men in the Fiery Furnace

Daniel 3

Shadrach, Meshach, and Abednego knew **God loved them.** They often prayed to God. One day, King Nebuchadnezzar told them to pray to a statue made of gold. The king said, "If you do not pray to the statue, I will kill you."

Shadrach, Meshach, and Abednego did not pray to the statue. They told King Nebuchadnezzar, "We will pray only to God. God is real. We will not pray to a piece of gold. Our God is able to save us. And even if He does not, we will not worship this false god." The three men refused to obey the king, and the king grew angry. He told his soldiers to throw the three men into a hot fire.

The king's soldiers threw Shadrach, Meshach, and Abednego into the fire. The furnace was so hot that the soldiers dropped over dead. But the three men in the furnace didn't die. They were walking around. God sent an angel to protect them. Then the king knew that God loved these men. Shadrach, Meshach, and Abednego came out of the fire. They didn't even smell like smoke! God had protected them.

Ducks in Raincoats / Matthew 28:20b

A card store recently offered for sale a card with a picture of a duck wearing a yellow raincoat. Above the duck were the words: "Into each life some rain will fall." The inside of the card said, "It's the sudden storms we can do without!" Ducks don't mind water, but stormy winds and lightning are dangerous.

Has it ever rained on a special event in your life? Maybe it was a ball game, a picnic, or your birthday. Maybe it rained every day on your vacation. If so, did you feel like a duck needing a raincoat?

The little duck on the card was overcome by a storm. Stormy problems come into our lives too—not just the drizzle of a little problem, but also the frightening power of big thunder boomers. We could lose a friend, move to a new school, become seriously ill, or even experience the death of someone we dearly love. Sometimes, a "storm" may be the feeling that nobody understands or cares about our problems.

Where is God when "storms" of fear, sadness, or loss overwhelm us? Is He there? Does He know? Does He care? Yes, God knows and cares. God is there. We can find Him in His Word. We can find Him in Baptism and in the Lord's Supper. He promises to be with us always, to the very end of the age. Through Jesus' suffering, death, and resurrection, God has given us His victory over the "storms" of sin and death. It doesn't matter what "stormy" problems come our way; we have a God who is with us.

Talk about it: Make a list of some of the "stormy" problems in your life. How has God been with you?

Prayer: Dear God, You care so much for me and have power to control absolutely everything that frightens me. Take care of me during life's "storms," and give me Your peace. In Jesus' name I pray. Amen.

God Saves Daniel from the Lions | Daniel 6

Daniel worked for King Darius. The king did not believe in God, but Daniel did. God had made Daniel wise and had given him faith. King Darius gave Daniel an important job. Daniel did everything well, and God blessed his work.

The king's other workers grew jealous. They wanted to kill Daniel. They told King Darius, "Make a new law. Everyone must pray to you. They may not pray to anyone else. If they do, they will be thrown into a lions' den!"

King Darius made this new law. Daniel still prayed to God. Some men saw him and sent him to the king. The king was sad. He liked Daniel. But he said, "I must obey my own law. Throw Daniel into the lions' den because he has broken my law." The king's men obeyed. Everyone was sure that hungry lions would kill Daniel. King Darius was upset. He did not eat or sleep that night.

The next morning, the king went to the lions' den. Daniel was still alive! Daniel said, "My God sent His angel, and he shut the mouths of the lions. They have not hurt me." The king was happy for Daniel. The king knew that God saved Daniel. He made a new law. He said that everyone in his kingdom must respect God. God delivered Daniel from the evil he faced in the den of lions. God has also delivered us from evil when He sent Jesus to save us from our sins.

Bitten / 2 Thessalonians 3:3

At the church camping trip, families gathered at the lake to talk and laugh. Hikes were taken in the autumn wonder. Bibles were opened to study. Tents popped up like tiny mountains. Lights were strung from campers' awnings. Coolers and lawn chairs cluttered the grassy areas.

The children ran, climbed, swam, and squealed. Delight turned to terror when Heidi screamed, "A snake! A snake! It bit me!" Friends rushed to help. Heidi's dad checked her ankle and found the puncture marks. Other parents grabbed lanterns, searched, and found the poisonous copperhead.

Heidi was taken to a nearby hospital and examined by a doctor. There, she received the snake-bite serum and was delivered from the poisonous bite.

When we pray the Lord's Prayer, we ask that God "deliver us from evil." But what kind of evil are we talking about? The evil we speak of in the Lord's Prayer is much like a poisonous snake bite. It comes from the devil and has come into the world as a result of sin.

These "poisonous bites" of evil are designed to hurt us in body and soul, possessions and property. The Lord helps us overcome the venom of the "poisonous bites" that the devil and our own sin bring into our lives. The Lord helps us endure the loss of friends, the disappointment of failures, and the painful results of sinful choices we have made.

Christ Jesus forgives our sinful choices. His grace delivers us from the poisonous bite of sin, death, and the devil.

Talk about it: Has anything evil ever happened to you? Have you ever been tempted to do evil to others? How can you resist those temptations?

Prayer: Dear God, deliver me from every evil through Jesus Christ, my Lord and Savior. Amen.

Through love serve one another.
Galatians 5:13

Esther Saves Her People | Esther 5–6

Long ago, the people of God were living in a faraway land. God had allowed them to be taken to this land because they continued to worship other gods. God wanted them to turn to Him once again for help.

The ruler of this land, King Ahasuerus, set out in search of a queen. Esther was chosen. Esther was one of the people of God. She had been raised by her uncle Mordecai. Mordecai also believed in the true God.

Mordecai refused to bow down to a high official named Haman. This made Haman angry. In fact, Haman was so angry at Mordecai he wanted to destroy not only Mordecai but all of God's people.

Mordecai told Esther to go to the king to ask that God's people be spared. Mordecai told Esther that she may have become queen for this reason, so she would be in position to help her people.

Esther obeyed Mordecai and went before the king. In those days, anyone who came before the king without being invited might be sentenced to death, even the king's wife! When the king saw Esther, however, he held out his golden scepter. This meant that Esther was welcome before the king and would not be killed. Esther told the king what Haman was doing. She pleaded with the king for the lives of her people. The king honored Esther's request, and God's people were saved. Esther did the difficult thing. She risked her life in order to plead for her people.

In a way, Esther reminds us of Jesus. Jesus risked His life to save us and all people. But Jesus did more than risk His life—He gave His life on the cross to save us!

Helping Others / 1 Thessalonians 5:9–11

It was the first game of the St. John girls' basketball season. Every girl on the team wore a look of defeat. After three minutes of play, the coach could see that something was wrong. She called a time-out to discuss the problem.

"What's going on out there?" asked the coach as the girls gathered around her.

"It's the other team," said Cathy. "They're saying things to us."

"Yeah," said Amy, "they're saying mean things."

"And calling us dirty names," added Erin.

"Well, girls," said the coach, "you know what they're doing. They're trying to distract you so your mind is not on the game. And it seems to be working. What do you think we should do?"

"I know what we should do," said Katelyn enthusiastically. "Let's pretend we don't even hear what they're saying. And let's talk more to one another to encourage one another in the plays."

"You're right, Katelyn," Cathy agreed. "We can turn this thing around. We can think really hard about our plays and concentrate on our shots."

"That sounds really great, girls," agreed the coach. "Now, let's ask God to help us do those things and get back out there and try to get a victory."

The team bowed their heads. "Lord, here we are in the middle of this game. Help us to do what You would have us do and act as You would have us act as we play. Help us to ignore and forgive the other team members for the wrong things they are doing. In Your name we pray. Amen."

The game did turn around from that point on. Later, when the game was over and the team members were congratulating one another in the dressing room, everyone agreed that it was Katelyn speaking up that saved the day.

Christians are a lot like the players on this basketball team. We sometimes find ourselves in difficult situations. At these times, we do well to remember that God has already won a great victory for us through His Son, Jesus Christ. By dying on the cross and rising again, Jesus has defeated our opponents—sin, death, and the devil. He wants us to share in the victory with Him in heaven. Like Katelyn on this team, and like Queen Esther long ago, we can serve Jesus by speaking the truth for the benefit of others as we have the opportunity. When we stay focused on God, we share the victory Christ has already won for us.

Talk about it: What opportunities to speak up to help others has God placed in your life?

 *Prayer: Dear Lord, thank You for winning the victory for me over sin, death, and the devil. Give me opportunities to speak up in order to help others. May the Holy Spirit give me strength to know what is the right thing to do and the courage to do it. In Your name I pray. Amen.*

Bless the LORD, O you His angels,
you mighty ones who do His Word,
obeying the voice of His Word!
Bless the LORD, all His hosts,
His ministers, who do His will!
Psalm 103:20–21

Angel Announcements | Luke 2:1–20

The Bible tells us that there are both good and bad angels. The bad angels serve Satan. They lead us to disobey God. But good angels serve God, and there are many of them. Good angels protect people from harm. The Bible also tells of many times when God sent His angels to bring messages to His people.

The coming of the Savior had been foretold throughout the Old Testament by the prophets. But when the time came for Jesus to be born, God sent His angels with important messages for those who would play important parts in the gift of God's Son to the world.

This is how the birth of the Savior came to be: The angel Gabriel appeared to Mary, a young woman of Nazareth who was engaged to be married to a carpenter named Joseph. The angel told Mary that she would have a child, the Son of God.

God also sent an angel to tell Joseph about this miraculous event. Both Joseph and Mary listened to the angel and believed the message from God the angel brought them. Joseph took Mary with him when he was required to go to Bethlehem, the town from which their ancestors came.

While in Bethlehem, Mary's baby, Jesus our Savior, was born. Because there was no room in the inn, baby Jesus was born in a place where animals were kept. His mother laid Him in a manger. An animal's feed box was the first crib for the Savior of the world.

Angels announced the Savior's birth to some shepherds and proclaimed, "Glory to God in the highest." The shepherds came to worship baby Jesus. When they left, they told everyone the good news that the Savior had been born!

Meet Ike / Psalm 91:11–12

Ike is a special kind of dog with a very important job. Ike is a leader dog who helps and protects a person with physical challenges. Maybe you have noticed Seeing Eye dogs with people who are blind, guiding them down the sidewalk or helping them cross busy streets. Ike is similar, but his human can see.

Ike is large, black, and furry, and he helps a woman in a motorized wheelchair. Everywhere the woman goes, Ike is sure to be by her side. When she goes to church, Ike goes too. When they go to a party, Ike gets dressed up and comes along. He is usually the center of attention.

When Ike goes out in public, he is working. He shouldn't be petted or distracted from his job of keeping guard. Ike knows that his duty is to protect and serve his human.

Thinking about how Ike does his job can remind us of God's angels. God created angels to serve Him and to help us. In the Bible, God used angels to announce important events such as the birth of Jesus (Luke 1:26–38; Matt. 1:18–21). God also uses angels to guard and protect His people, even though we can't see them (Psalm 91:11–12). Angels are a part of God's constant care for us, His beloved children.

God's good angels are many and powerful, but the Bible tells us that evil angels also exist in the world. Satan and the evil angels try to trick us, trap us, and deceive us. But Jesus is always more powerful, and He assures us of His victory over Satan. Each temptation is a trick of the devil, but through His Word and in Baptism, God strengthens us to say no to sin by His power. God forgives our sins and protects us from evil.

~~~~~~~~~~

Talk about it: How is Ike like an angel? When do you think God has protected you?

 *Prayer: Dear God, thank You for Your angels. I know You will always watch over me. Protect me in all my ways until I live with You in heaven. In the name of Jesus I pray. Amen.*

[Jesus] became flesh and dwelt among us, and we have seen His glory, glory as of the only Son from the Father, full of grace and truth. John 1:14

Jesus Is Born in Bethlehem | Luke 2:1–20

Mary and Joseph were glad to reach their destination. It was hard to travel from Nazareth to Bethlehem. Mary was very tired. She was expecting a baby at any time. Mary and Joseph had to go to Bethlehem to be counted. The government wanted to know how many people lived in the country. Mary and Joseph looked for a place to stay. Nobody had room. Finally, they were allowed to rest in a stable, which is a place where people keep animals.

That night, Jesus was born. Angels sang songs to some shepherds. They were happy to hear about Jesus, the newborn Savior. The angels told them where they could find the baby.

"Here He is!" shouted the shepherds. Mary and Joseph kneeled next to baby Jesus. The baby rested in a manger. The shepherds were the first to see God's Son. They were so excited! On their way back, they told other people about Jesus.

This was a great day! People had waited for Jesus for many years. God had promised that the

Savior would take away their sins. God wanted the world to know about Jesus. He wanted people to be saved from their sins. That is why He sent Jesus.

How could such a little baby help us, we may wonder. But Jesus was no ordinary baby. Even though He was born like any other human baby, He is also the Son of God. He grew up like other children grow up. He knew times of happiness and sadness. He felt hungry, wet, and cold, just as we sometimes do. He lived life in our place, without sin. He also died for us, taking our place on the cross to pay for our sins.

God Does the Unexpected / John 1:14

Which animal would you expect to win a race—a rabbit or a turtle? A rabbit is much faster, of course. But remember the fable of the tortoise and the hare? The rabbit was too sure of himself and wasted time along the way. The turtle won.

Would you choose a big engine or a little one to pull a train up a mountain? A children's story tells about a little engine that did the job. He believed he could do it.

Then there's the story of David and Goliath. No one except David believed he could defeat the giant. Yet, with God's help, he did exactly that.

Jesus' birth in a lowly stable was a surprise to many people.

Here was the long-awaited Son of God lying on straw. His parents were poor, not rich or important. There were smelly animals nearby. Why, there weren't even any baby clothes to put on Jesus!

As an adult, Jesus didn't always do what others expected. He spent much time with known sinners and people who weren't well liked. Many of the important religious leaders opposed Jesus, and at times, He was chased out of town. Even His own disciples wondered when Jesus would set up a kingdom on earth. He never did. Instead, He died like a criminal. We refer to this part of Jesus' life as His state of humili-

ation. Jesus humbled Himself to forgive and save us.

Still, Jesus' death accomplished the most important thing of all time. By it, our sins are forgiven. Our relationship with God is restored. We have been given eternal life. Who would ever have expected it to turn out that way?

The Bible is full of stories and events where God does the unexpected. Often, He chooses something or someone weak and lowly to do great things. That way, His great power and love are clear for all to see.

Talk about it: Make a list of some unexpected things about Jesus.

Prayer: I thank You, Lord, for humbling Yourself to forgive and save us. Give me faith to trust You when things seem impossible to me. In Your name I pray. Amen.

To Him who is able to do far more abundantly than all that we ask or think, according to the power at work within us, to Him be glory in the church and in Christ Jesus throughout all generations, forever and ever. Amen. Ephesians 3:20–21

Anna and Simeon See the Savior | Luke 2:22–38

God sent Jesus to be the Savior of the world. He was born on the first Christmas. When He was forty days old, Mary and Joseph took Him to the temple. They were obeying God. God wanted mothers and fathers to bring their children to Him.

A man named Simeon was in the temple. He believed God's promises of a Savior. God told Simeon he would live long enough to see Jesus. How happy he was when Mary and Joseph brought Jesus to the temple! Simeon knew that God had answered his prayer. He knew Jesus was the Savior.

Simeon held baby Jesus. He said, "Now I have peace. I have seen Jesus! He will save all people." Then Simeon blessed Mary and Joseph. He said that Jesus would do many things for all people.

Another person in the temple that day was an old woman named Anna. She prayed night and day in the temple. She wanted to see Jesus too. Anna came up to Mary, Joseph, and Jesus. She thanked God for the Savior. She thanked God for answering her prayer. Then she told people about Jesus. She said, "Jesus will save us." Simeon and Anna thanked and praised God for sending Jesus. They knew God answers prayers.

Pray without Fear / Psalm 19:14

Sunday School class was nearly over. "Christi, will you please say our closing prayer?" asked Mrs. Smith.

"Me? I don't know how to pray in front of people!" exclaimed Christi.

"Do you have any trouble talking to me?" asked the teacher.

"No," Christi answered.

"Then you won't have any problem talking to God. You see, Christi, God is our heavenly Father. He wants us to talk to Him just like we talk to our father and mother on earth. He wants to hear our words of thanks and praise for all He has given us and especially for the forgiveness of sins and salvation Jesus earned for us. He wants to hear about the things we would like to have for ourselves and for others. And He promises to hear and answer us.

Prayer is not about elegant words. It is conversation from your heart. God will always hear your prayers."

"Okay. I'll give it a try," said Christi.

~~~~~~~~~~~~~~~~~~~~

Talk about it: What answers has God given to the prayers you have prayed? How do you know that God cares about you enough to answer your prayers?

Prayer: Dear God, help us to talk to You regularly and often in prayer. Help us to share our joys and sorrows with You, even as we ask You for things we would like to have. We praise You, Lord, for Your forgiveness and salvation. In Jesus' name we pray. Amen.

"Honor your father and mother" (this is the first commandment with a promise), "that it may go well with you and that you may live long in the land." Ephesians 6:2–3

Jesus Grows Up | Luke 2:41–52

Mary and Joseph and Jesus made their home in Nazareth. When Jesus was twelve years old, He went with His parents to Jerusalem to celebrate the feast of the Passover. On the return trip, after they had journeyed for a day, Mary and Joseph discovered that Jesus was not with their group of family and friends. Anxiously, Mary and Joseph returned to Jerusalem to look for Jesus.

After three days, they found Him in the temple with the teachers of religion. He was listening to them and asking them questions. The teachers were amazed at Jesus' knowledge and understanding of God. Mary asked, "Son, why have You done this? Your father and I have been looking all over for You. We have been very worried."

Jesus said that He was in His Father's house doing His Father's business. Mary and Joseph didn't understand what He meant.

Jesus returned with Mary and Joseph to Nazareth. He obeyed His parents completely, because He is the Son of God and without sin. Jesus grew tall and wise, and He was loved by both God and other people.

Visiting Granny Annie / Mark 7:10

Hurry up," Mom called up the stairs. "We don't want to keep Granny Annie waiting."

Today was Granny Annie's ninetieth birthday. Kanesha and Kenny and Mom had planned a big celebration. Mom baked a cake, and the twins helped decorate it with candy. They could hardly wait for a taste!

Granny Annie wasn't really their grandmother, but they loved her just the same. She had lived in a home for retired teachers for a long time. The twins' mother, who was also a teacher, started visiting Granny Annie even before Kanesha and Kenny were born. So they had known her their whole life.

Once, they asked Mom why Granny Annie lived there. It was more like a dormitory or a hospital than a house. She moved there when she needed help, Mom explained. She sometimes forgot to take her medicine, so she couldn't live alone. But she had no relatives, and she needed others to care for her.

Some elderly people in nursing homes are not as fortunate as Granny Annie. They don't have anyone who comes to visit them. Sometimes they feel alone and forgotten.

Jesus honored and obeyed His parents. Jesus commands us to honor our parents and other authorities too. That can include all older people, and especially fellow Christians. The Good News about Jesus has been passed from one generation to the next. If older folks had not been faithful to God and faithful in telling His Word, we might not know about Jesus.

Talk about it: What are some ways we can show the love of Jesus to our parents? What are some ways we can show the love of Jesus to older people who are not our parents?

Prayer: Thank You, dear Lord, for the faithfulness of earlier generations. Help me to find ways to honor them, for Jesus' sake. Amen.

The grace of the Lord Jesus Christ and the love of God and the fellowship of the Holy Spirit be with you all.
2 Corinthians 13:14

Jesus Is Baptized by John the Baptist

Matthew 3

John the Baptist began his ministry in the desert. He preached, telling people to repent of their sins. John was preparing the way for the coming of the Savior. People came to John to be baptized. Jesus also came from Galilee to the Jordan River to be baptized. John, however, resisted, saying, "I need to be baptized by You. Why do You come to be baptized by me?"

Jesus answered, "It is necessary for Me to be baptized to fulfill all righteousness." So John baptized Jesus in the Jordan River.

When Jesus came out of the water, the heavens opened and the Holy Spirit descended on Jesus in the shape of a dove. A voice from heaven announced, "This is My beloved Son in whom I am well pleased." The voice from heaven was that of God the Father.

All three persons in the one true God can be seen and heard at Jesus' Baptism. Jesus is God the Son, the Holy Spirit descended upon Jesus as a dove, and the voice heard is that of God the Father in heaven.

The one true God is three persons in one divine being. This truth about God is revealed to us in God's Word, and we believe it, even though it is a mystery we don't understand completely.

God Is God / Isaiah 6:3

Marsha was ready for her turn to share her news. Her little brother was telling all about the numbers he learned at school. "One plus one equals two," he said proudly.

"That's right, Jeremy," Mom said. "Good for you."

"Want to know what I learned today?" asked Marsha. She looked at Jeremy to make sure he was listening. Then she looked at Mom and announced, "I learned that one plus one plus one equals . . . one!"

"No, it doesn't!" Jeremy blurted out.

"Wait a minute, Jeremy," said Mom. "Let Marsha explain. Marsha, when does one plus one plus one equal one?"

"Well I wasn't talking about math." Marsha smiled; she could tell her little brother was confused. "I was talking about God." Marsha explained, "There's God the Father, God the Son, and God the Holy Spirit. One plus one plus one.

But when you put them all together you still just have one God."

"Is that right, Mom?" Jeremy asked, still confused.

"Yes, Jeremy; that's right," answered Mom.

"But I still don't understand God," Marsha admitted.

Understanding God isn't always easy. God is different from us. We are people. God is God. He doesn't require that we understand everything about Him because, as humans, that would be impossible. God is greater than human minds can understand.

God does, however, require that we put Him—the Father, Son, and Holy Spirit—above all else in our lives. God created us, loves us, and cares for us. He asks that we acknowledge His love by loving Him in return. He wants us to love Him more than we love money, books, clothing, cartoons, Hollywood actors, or famous singers. God

even asks that we love and trust Him more than we love and trust our family and friends.

Do we always put God first? Of course not. People are sinful and fail to follow God's commands. But God is good. Even though we fail to love God, He never stops loving us. We are reminded by the Holy Spirit that God the Father loves us so much that He sent His Son, Jesus Christ, to die for our sins and forgive us for breaking His Commandments. What an awesome God we have, who loves and forgives us even when we forget to love Him in return!

Talk about it: Only one God exists, and that true God is the Father, Son, and Holy Spirit. Because we are human, we cannot understand how God can be three in one. But we know it's true because the Bible says so. Read about Jesus' Baptism in Matthew 3:16–17, and review the way the three persons of God reveal themselves.

Prayer: Dear God—Father, Son, and Holy Spirit—thank You for being such a wonderful God. Help me to fear, love, and trust in You above all things. Amen.

So by the one man's obedience the many will
be made righteous. Romans 5:19

Jesus Is Tempted in the Wilderness | Matthew 4:1–11

When Jesus grew up and became a man, the devil tempted Him to sin, just as the devil tempted Adam and Eve in the Garden of Eden. The devil knew that if he could get Jesus to sin, Jesus would not be able to save us.

Jesus went into the wilderness, where He went without food for forty days. During this time, the devil tempted Jesus to prove He is God's Son by turning the stones into bread and eating the bread. But Jesus used God's Word to counter the devil's tempting.

Next, the devil took Jesus to the top of the temple. He told Jesus to throw Himself down from the temple and not to worry because God's angels would keep Him safe. Again, Jesus used God's Word against the devil and did not do what the devil told Him to.

Then the devil led Jesus to a high mountain and promised to give Jesus all the kingdoms of the world if Jesus would bow and worship Him. One more time, Jesus used God's Word against the devil.

Three times the devil tempted Jesus, and three times Jesus resisted him. Jesus did God's will instead of the devil's will. Jesus obeyed God in our place in order to save us.

Sometime later, Jesus defeated the devil once and for all when He died in our place on the cross. There, Jesus took the punishment we deserve because of our sins. Three days later, Jesus rose again from the dead, showing that He has power even over death. One day, Jesus will return to raise from the dead all who died believing in Him and will grant them and all living believers eternal life in heaven.

Relief Pitcher / Galatians 3:13

Uncle Pete, I'm sorry you saw me pitch such a lousy game." Jason had invited Uncle Pete to come to his game, but then he pitched the worst game of his life.

"It's okay, buddy." Uncle Pete put his arm around Jason. "Remember, your team still won. Your relief pitcher had an amazing game."

"I know," said Jason, "I can't believe how well he played! Thanks to me, we were down 4 to 1, and then he came in and didn't let anyone else score."

"And on top of all that, he scored a grand slam to win the game 5 to 4," chuckled Uncle Pete. "Man, that was fun to watch."

"Our relief pitcher saved the game, that's for sure," said Jason.

"Do you know who the all-time greatest relief pitcher is?" asked Uncle Pete.

"No, who?"

"Jesus of Nazareth."

Jason laughed. "Jesus played baseball?"

"Think about it, Jason. When we try to win the game of life by ourselves, we lose every time to Satan. He is stronger and smarter than we are. But Jesus is like our relief pitcher. When He died on the cross, He took our place against Satan's evil team. He struck out the evil ones and threw Satan out of the game. Best of all, He hit the grand-slam home run to win it all when He rose from the grave on Easter morning. That's our victory too!"

"Yeah, it does feel good to be on the winning team."

"With Jesus as your relief pitcher, you're on the winning team every day!"

Jesus did all the work for us. He took our place on the cross, even though we all deserve the punishment for our sin. Christ's death and resurrection is the only way we win!

Talk about it: Why do we need a relief pitcher to win the victory over sin, death, and the devil?

Prayer: Dear Jesus, thank You for taking our place in the game of life and striking out Satan. We could never win without You. In Your name we pray. Amen.

God so loved the world, that He gave His only Son, that whoever believes in Him should not perish but have eternal life. John 3:16

Jesus Teaches Nicodemus | John 3:1–21

Nicodemus was a teacher. Many of his friends didn't believe that Jesus was the Promised Savior. But Nicodemus believed in Jesus. He had seen Jesus do miracles. Now he wanted to know more about Jesus. Nicodemus had many questions.

Jesus told Nicodemus, "No one can see the kingdom of God unless he is born again." Nicodemus didn't understand. He asked, "How can a person be born a second time?" Jesus said, "You are born again when you are baptized and receive forgiveness and faith." This surprised Nicodemus. He thought people could get into God's kingdom by being good.

Jesus told Nicodemus that no one could ever be that good! He said that faith and forgiveness were God's gifts. God's kingdom was a gift.

Nicodemus listened as Jesus talked. He was the first person to hear these famous words of Jesus: "God so loved the world, that He gave His only Son, that whoever believes in Him should not perish but have eternal life." Jesus said that He was God's Son.

Jesus wanted Nicodemus to be in God's kingdom. He wanted Nicodemus to know and believe the Gospel. The word *Gospel* means "good news." The good news for us and all people is that God loved the world so much that He sent His only Son to earn salvation for all people.

A Clear Message / Colossians 1:13–14

Mitchell's mom planned a fun-filled party for his birthday. All afternoon, Mitchell's friends played games and won prizes.

"Now," said Mitchell's mom, "the last game is a treasure hunt. I'll give you the first clue, and you have to use the information I give you to find the next clue. Keep finding more clues and you'll come to the treasure. Have fun."

Some of the clues were easy. Others were tricky, and the boys and girls whooped and cheered when they finally solved them. They knew they were getting near the end. But there was a problem with the last clue. The words on the paper were smeared.

The message wasn't clear, and Mitchell and his friends didn't know what they were supposed to do. How could they ever reach the treasure?

Thankfully, God's most important messages to us are very clear. In the Ten Commandments, God tells us things such as not to kill, not to steal, and not to use His name in cursing. But God also clearly tells us that we are sinners who cannot keep God's Law perfectly.

God is very clear as He tells us how He takes away our sin. He says in John 3:16 that He loved the world so much that He gave His only Son, that whoever believes in Him will not die! That's pretty clear, isn't it? In that short verse, God tells us why and how we are saved. It is a message that gives us the greatest treasure—eternal life with God in heaven.

~~~~~~~~~~~~~~~~

Talk about it: Why do we need the Gospel?

 *Prayer: Dear heavenly Father, thank You for being very clear about how people can be saved. Thank You for sending Jesus. Amen.*

And there is salvation in no one else, for there is no other name under heaven given among men by which we must be saved. Acts 4:12

Jesus Forgives the Woman at the Well

John 4:1–44

Once when Jesus was traveling with His disciples, they passed through the country of Samaria. Jesus had become tired from the trip and sat down to rest at a well. Here, He met a woman from a nearby town who had come to get some water from the well.

The Jewish people were not friendly with the people of Samaria. And in those days, teachers like Jesus did not speak with women in public. But Jesus spoke to this woman.

He talked with her about her sins and her need for a Savior. Then Jesus told her He was the promised one who had come to save all people from their sins.

The woman went back to her town and told her friends and neighbors about Jesus. And they too came to believe in Him as the Son of God and Savior of the world.

No Need for Extra Credit / Ephesians 2:8–9

"Are you saved?" asked one of Micah's friends.

"Yes, I am," Micah quickly replied. "Are you saved?"

"Well, not yet, but I will be next year," replied eleven-year old Kurt.

"Do you believe in Jesus as your Savior, Kurt?" Micah asked.

"Oh, yes," was his immediate response.

"Then you are saved," Micah assured him. "Jesus has forgiven your sins and will take you to heaven."

Kurt smiled with happiness. Kurt had been baptized, but he still felt that he had more things to do before he could be saved. But the Bible tells us, "For by grace you have been saved through faith. And this is not your own doing; it is the gift of God, not a result of works, so that no one may boast" (Ephesians 2:8–9). No one can earn extra credit (or any credit at all) to get into heaven. Jesus has done it all. His death paid for our sins, totally and forever. When we say, "I believe . . . in Jesus Christ, His only Son, our Lord," we are confessing to ourselves and to others that we believe in Jesus as our Savior, the one who has saved us. Faith in Him is all we need in order to say, "Yes, I am saved!"

This good news can put an eternal smile on the faces of your friends and neighbors. There is no list of things to do before you can become a Christian. There is no waiting for salvation. Boldly and quickly, we can tell the worried world, "Believe in the Lord Jesus, and you will be saved" (Acts 16:31).

Talk about it: What does it mean to be saved? What could you say to someone who tells you that he or she is not yet saved?

Prayer: Lord Jesus, what a mighty God and Savior You are! Thank You for living and dying for me. Thank You for the salvation that I have in You. Help me always to trust in You. Help me to tell others about You and Your saving love. I pray this in Your holy name. Amen.

[Jesus] is before all things, and in Him all things hold together. Colossians 1:17

Jesus Calms the Storm | Matthew 8:23–27

Jesus was tired. He had healed many people earlier that day. Now He needed to rest. Jesus said to His disciples, "Let's go to the other side of the lake." So they got into a boat and began to sail. Jesus fell asleep. A sudden strong storm did not wake Him. Waves crashed over the boat. The disciples were afraid that the boat would tip over and they would die. Jesus just kept on sleeping.

"How can He sleep in this storm?" asked the disciples. They cried, "Wake up, Jesus! We are going to die!" Jesus got up. He looked at the storm and said, "Quiet! Be still!" The wind stopped blowing. The waves stopped crashing. Then Jesus asked, "Why are you afraid? Don't you trust God?"

The disciples were afraid again. They asked, "Who is this that even the wind and the waves obey Him?" The answer is this: Jesus is God. The Lord God has all of nature under His control. God made the world, and God continues to take care of us. What a great and awesome God He is!

Find the letters of the word "live" in the word "believe." Why is it important to live, as well as to believe, God's Word?

Never Beyond God's Care / Romans 8:38

A fisherman once lived in a house by the sea. Each day, he sailed his small boat out to sea to catch fish to sell. One day, the fisherman stayed out too late, and a sudden storm darkened the sky. Before he knew it, he couldn't see the shore. The frightened fisherman didn't know which direction to sail. What if he went the wrong way and sailed farther out to sea? He prayed hard that God would guide him home.

After a while, the fisherman saw a light flickering in the distance. Yes! It seemed to be getting brighter. He set off in the direction of the glowing light and soon reached the shore. How thankful he was!

But then the fisherman discovered a horrible thing. The light that had guided him back to shore was a fire that burned down his house. The fire that saved his life destroyed his home and all his possessions.

Sometimes, it seems that things can't get any worse. Earthquakes, hurricanes, floods, or tornados may destroy everything we have. Sickness, divorce, money problems, or abuse can ruin lives. Tragedies and suffering are a result of sin in the world. As long as we live in this sinful world, there will be hard times, suffering, and death. Still, God never loosens His control over all things. We can rely on His unchanging, unending love for us, no matter what happens.

In times of trouble, we can count on God to be the one treasure we will never lose. Nothing can separate us from the love of God. We can be sure of that because He loved us enough to send His Son to rescue us from sin.

Jesus lost a lot too. He gave up His place in heaven to live on earth. He felt sadness and weariness, and He was treated unfairly. He even lost His life when He died a horrible death on the cross. To people watching that, it must have seemed there was no hope.

But through His death and resurrection, Jesus proved that He has power over sin and death! We now have a new life in Christ. We can trust His promise always to be with us and to give us what we need, even when times get tough. We can always look to Him for a new beginning.

Talk about it: Have you ever felt as though things in your life could not get worse? How did Jesus help you through it?

Prayer: Heavenly Father, help us to remember that even though bad things happen in our sinful world, we are never outside of Jesus' love and care for us. We pray in His name. Amen.

[Jesus said,] "I am the bread of life." John 6:35

Jesus Feeds Five Thousand | Matthew 14:13–21

Where will we get food to feed all these people?" asked the disciples. They were worried. More than five thousand people sat on the grass. They wanted to hear Jesus teach. They wanted to see Jesus do miracles. They were hungry too. There was no place to buy food. Jesus wanted to feed the people.

Jesus told His disciples to get some food. The disciples didn't know what to do. That much food would cost too much, and they were far from the markets. One disciple found a boy who had brought his lunch. He had two small fish and five little loaves of bread. The disciples knew it wasn't enough to feed five thousand people, but they showed the lunch to Jesus anyway.

Jesus prayed. Then He said, "Pass around the food." Jesus broke off pieces of bread and fish. Then He broke off more . . . and still more. He never ran out of food. All the people ate as much as they wanted. The disciples even had twelve baskets of leftovers.

Jesus wanted the people to know that He is truly God. Providing food for five thousand people was wonderful, but His best miracle was still to come. Soon, He would die on the cross and arise at Easter to save us. Faith in Jesus' death and resurrection to earn us forgiveness, new life, and salvation is all we need in order to be spiritually alive, well-fed, and healthy. That is why Jesus calls Himself the living bread.

The Living Bread / John 6:51

Juan had just come in from playing baseball. "What's for supper, Mom?" asked Juan. Juan had been playing all afternoon, and he was hungry.

"Tonight, we are having your favorite meal: fried chicken with mashed potatoes and gravy!" Mom informed him cheerfully.

After washing his hands, Juan came to the kitchen, and they began to eat. Juan didn't say much during supper. He was too busy eating. He asked for seconds. And then he asked for one more helping still. "Wow, that was good, Mom!" Juan praised. "But I am so full, I don't know if I will ever be hungry again."

"Oh, you will," Mom countered. "You'll be plenty hungry tomorrow. But your comment reminds me of something Jesus said once. 'I am the bread of life,' He told His followers. 'Whoever feeds on this bread will live forever.' I think about these words of Jesus sometimes when I am at the altar receiving the Lord's Supper."

"How does the Lord's Supper feed you so that you live forever, Mom?"

"That's a good question, Juan. It's the forgiveness and salvation I receive in the Lord's Supper that assures me I will live forever. With the bread and wine at this special meal, I receive Jesus' body and blood for the forgiveness of my sins and the assurance that Jesus has saved me eternally."

"I'm glad I know Jesus," Juan replied.

"I'm glad I know Him too" said Mom. "Now, do you think you might be interested in some dessert?"

Talk about it: Why is the Lord's Supper such a special meal?

Prayer: Dear God, You have forgiven my sins through Jesus. Plus, You have brought me to faith in You. Feed me on God's Word so that I may live with You forever. I pray in Jesus' name. Amen.

The Transfiguration of Jesus | 2 Peter 1:16–21

After seeing Jesus rise up into heaven, Peter, one of Jesus' followers, wrote about the things he had heard and seen concerning Jesus. He wrote about a time when Jesus was with Peter, James, and John. Suddenly, Jesus began to become very bright and to shine. Jesus shone brightly to show that He is God. While Peter and the others were watching Jesus at this special moment, a voice from heaven spoke and said about Jesus, "This is My beloved Son, with whom I am well pleased." This voice was the voice of God the Father. So, Jesus is God, and the Father in heaven is also God. Peter went on to write about the Spirit of God. Peter's words tell us about the work of the Holy Spirit. The Spirit gives people the words of the Bible. From other places in the Bible, we know that the Holy Spirit works through God's Word to give us faith and to keep us in the faith. So, Jesus is God, the Heavenly Father is God, and the Holy Spirit is God. There are three persons in one God. We learn about all three in the Bible. Because the Holy Spirit inspired people to write the Bible, we call it the Holy Scriptures.

Who Wrote It? / 2 Timothy 3:21

You probably know the nursery rhyme "Mary Had a Little Lamb." But do you know who wrote it? The answer would depend on whom you ask. The people of Sterling, Massachusetts, believe it was written by John Roulston. He was a classmate of Mary Sawyer, who he claimed was the girl whose lamb followed her to school.

But the residents of Newport, New Hampshire, don't agree. They say the poem was written by Sarah Hale. It was first published in a book of children's poems in 1830.

Who really wrote "Mary Had a Little Lamb"? Was it the child John Roulston? Or was it grown-up Sarah Hale? We will probably never know for sure. The poem was written over 150 years ago, so it's not easy to find the answer.

We can ask the same question about the Bible. Who wrote it? Was it many different people writing what they thought was true? Peter gives us the answer. He says, "Men spoke from God as they were carried along by the Holy Spirit." People did the writing, but the Holy Spirit told them what to say. We call the Bible the "Holy Scriptures" because it was written by the Holy Spirit through men. The Bible is the divine Word of God.

It really isn't important to know who wrote "Mary Had a Little Lamb." But it is important for us to know who wrote the Bible. People sometimes make mistakes when they write, but the Holy Spirit never makes mistakes. Because the Holy Spirit is God, we can believe what He tells us in the Bible's words.

Talk about it: People often call the Bible the "Holy Scriptures." What other names for the Bible can you think of? Why do you think people sometimes use these other names for the Bible?

Prayer: My Savior, how glad I am that I can believe every word of the Bible! Thank You for Your Holy Word. Amen.

Jesus Teaches Martha and Mary | Luke 10:38–42

Jesus was often a guest at the home of two sisters, Mary and Martha, and their brother Lazarus. They lived in Bethany, a tiny village not far from Jerusalem. While on His way to Jerusalem, Jesus often stopped to visit with His friends. Once when Jesus came to visit, Martha kept busy working around the house getting things ready to serve Jesus. Mary, on the other hand, remained with Jesus, listening to His words. Martha asked Jesus, "Lord, don't You care that my sister has left me to do the work by myself? Ask her to help me."

Jesus answered her, "Martha, Martha, you are worried and upset about many things, but only one thing is needed. Mary has chosen what is better, and it will not be taken away from her."

The one thing Mary had chosen was to hear God's Word. Like Martha, we can let things get in the way of hearing God's Word. We can think about other things while the pastor is teaching us from God's Word. We can do other things on Sunday morning instead of going to church. But God's Spirit helps us to choose what is better, just as Mary did.

Which One? / Colossians 3:16

Aunt Jen always gives the best gifts, thought Alana as she struggled with the wrapping paper. She couldn't wait to get her birthday present open.

The wrappings fell to the floor. Alana fought to hide her disappointment. "It's a Bible," said Alana, trying to sound pleased. Her mom could tell she wasn't too happy.

"You can read a chapter or two each day," suggested Mom.

Weeks went by. Alana hadn't taken the time to read her new Bible. One rainy day, a bored Alana finally took the thick book off the shelf in her room. She thumbed through the pages and, to her surprise, an envelope slipped out from the pages of the Bible and landed in her lap. Inside the envelope was a fifty-dollar bill, along with a note from Aunt Jen.

"Dear Alana," the note said, "I hope you enjoy your two gifts. Let me know which one you think is more valuable."

Alana thought about the gifts from Aunt Jen. It would be fun to buy a new game or bracelet with the money. And to think, Alana had almost missed out on being able to spend it.

But Alana almost missed out on a much more important gift. The Bible contains many wonderful messages from God, written especially for us. In the Third Commandment, God asks that we gladly hear, learn, and think about His Word often. From the creation story to Jesus' death and resurrection to the promise of life in heaven, God's Word is a gift to be treasured.

The next day, Alana wrote a letter: "Dear Aunt Jen, Thank you for your two wonderful gifts. I spent my money on a game I had been wanting for a long time, and I've just started reading my Bible every day. You asked me to tell you which gift is more valuable. Here's what I think . . ."

Talk about it: How do you think Alana finished the letter to Aunt Jen?

Prayer: Dear God, thank You for the Bible. Open my eyes and ears as I read and hear Your Word, which leads me closer to Jesus, my Savior. Amen.

Call upon Me in the day of trouble; I will deliver you, and you shall glorify Me. Psalm 50:15

Jesus Heals a Gentile Woman's Daughter

Matthew 15:21–28

Jesus traveled throughout the land, preaching the Good News of salvation. He healed the sick, and He instructed those who, like His disciples, came to believe in Him as the Son of God and the Savior of the world. When Jesus came to the coastal region of Tyre and Sidon, a woman of Canaan—a Gentile—came to Him and pleaded with Him, saying, "Have mercy on me, O Lord, Son of David! My daughter is possessed by a demon."

Jesus did not respond to the woman, and His disciples begged Him to send her away. But Jesus spoke to her, "I have been sent only to the house of Israel," He said.

But the woman knelt before Jesus, insisting. She continued to pray, "Lord, help me."

Jesus answered, "It is not fair to take the children's bread and throw it to the dogs."

"Yes, Lord," the woman countered, "but even the dogs eat the crumbs that fall from their masters' table."

Then Jesus said to her, "Woman, you have great faith! Your request is granted." And instantly, the woman's daughter was healed.

The Line Is Open / 1 Thessalonians 5:16–18

Marcus impatiently dialed the phone for the fifth time. He held his breath as he waited for the ring. The line was still busy, and since Grandfather had no answering machine, he couldn't leave a message. Angry and disappointed, Marcus hung up the phone. He really wanted to talk to Grandfather about the trouble he was having at school. Grandfather always had time to listen, but not now. Today, his phone was busy.

Marcus paced around the living room, trying to think of someone he could talk to. His father was on a business trip; his mother wouldn't be home until late, and his friends wouldn't be able to help him with this problem.

On his third cycle around the living room, Marcus paused in front of a picture of Jesus. As he stood there, he could hear in his mind Grandfather saying, "Marcus, remember that you're never alone. You can always talk to Jesus. You can count on Him to hear your prayer."

Jesus always has a clear "phone" line. He died to take away the barriers created by our sins. Now, we have instant access to our Lord at all times though prayer. We can pray standing up, sitting down, kneeling, at school, in bed, at the table, during a test, on an airplane, alone, with a friend, at three o'clock in the morning, at ten o'clock at night—anywhere, anytime.

How does God answer us when we pray? He answers our prayers in His own time and in His own special way. Sometimes, God answers our prayers through the Bible, and sometimes through other people. Sometimes, He answers with the weather, and some-times through a miracle. God is all-powerful, and He answers prayers in all kinds of ways. But we can be certain of one thing—He *always* answers. And He answers in the way that is best and at the right time.

Like Marcus, we can talk to our Savior when we're having trouble at school or at home. We can also thank Him for fun times and good friends. We can tell Him that we love drawing or jumping or swimming, and we can thank Him for giving us strong minds and bodies. Whenever we need help and guidance, Jesus asks that we pray to Him for support.

~~~~~~~~~~~~~~~~~~

Talk about it: Read Romans 8:26. Who helps us pray? How is His help reassuring?

Prayer: Dear Savior, help me to remember that You can always be reached and that You're never too busy when I call You. I know that You will hear and answer my every prayer. In Jesus' name I pray. Amen.

[Jesus said,] "I am the good shepherd.
I know My own and My own know Me."
John 10:14

Jesus Is the Good Shepherd | John 10:1–21

Jesus sometimes used word pictures to teach **people important truths.** For example, when Jesus was talking about the Church, He used the word picture of sheep and their shepherd. Jesus said that He is like a good shepherd, because a good shepherd would give his life to save the sheep, just as Jesus would give His very life to save each of us. Jesus said that He is the only one who can keep people safe. He is the only one who can lead people to heaven. There is no other way. People who believe in Jesus follow Him.

Just as a sheepfold has many different kinds of sheep, including young and old, tall and short, cautious and adventuresome, the Church has many different types of people. But Jesus, our Savior, knows each of us; He calls us by name. And, as members of His Church on earth, we follow Him. Since we follow the Good Shepherd, Jesus, He would have us love and care for others in the flock in the same ways that He loves and cares for each of us.

All Part of the Picture / Romans 12:4–5

"All right, class," Mrs. Sanchez said, "Time for art!"

Art was Roxanne's favorite subject. She quickly cleared her desk. Mrs. Sanchez gave a blank sheet of paper and a small box of crayons to each student. "Today, I want you to draw a landscape using the crayons I gave you. Let's get started."

This'll be easy, Roxanne thought. But when she opened the box of crayons, she saw that each one of them was exactly the same shade of blue. How could she draw a landscape with one color? Looking around, Roxanne noticed that all of her classmates were looking at their boxes of crayons in confusion.

Roxanne raised her hand. "Mrs. Sanchez, all I have is blue. I could color in the sky, but that's about it."

"Hmm." Mrs. Sanchez placed one finger on her chin and looked up at the ceiling in thought. Then she said, "You know, you may have to find the color you need from someone else. I think the only way you'll be able to finish your picture is by working together."

Have you ever been faced with a problem that you tried to take care of on your own, but you just couldn't? God has given each one of us special talents and strengths. What's easy for you might be quite difficult for me, and vice versa. God has surrounded us with friends and family who help us when we need it. In the Church, He has given us brothers and sisters in Christ. And I'm not just talking about your home congregation.

The Holy Christian Church is made up of every person who believes in Jesus as his or her Savior. All of us are unique—we have differing strengths and weaknesses, different cultural backgrounds, and unique talents. But all believers have one thing in common: Jesus Christ.

As believers, we are part of the Holy Christian Church, which means that we all are saved by Jesus. Like a good shepherd who gave His life for His sheep, Jesus died and rose again so that those who have faith in Him can have eternal life. What a beautiful picture!

Talk about it: Think about a few ways that you can serve Jesus as a member of His Church. How can you help add more members?

Prayer: Dear God, thank You for filling the world with other believers. Help us to support one another as we live together as Your people. Help us to grow Your Church by sending Your Holy Spirit so that more people can be brought to faith. In Jesus' name we pray. Amen.

The Parable of the Rich Man and Lazarus

Luke 16:19–31

Jesus once told a story about a certain rich man who lived in luxury, clothed in purple and fine linen, who enjoyed good food and the best of everything every day. He also told about a certain poor man named Lazarus who was full of sores and who laid at the rich man's gate. Dogs came and licked Lazarus's sores. Lazarus would gladly have eaten the crumbs that fell from the rich man's table.

Jesus said that when Lazarus died, the angels carried him to heaven to the company of Abraham. When the rich man died, the angels did not carry him to heaven. In hell, he looked up in pain and suffering and saw Lazarus the beggar resting happily with Abraham. The rich man cried, "Father Abraham, have mercy on me and send Lazarus to dip the end of his finger in water and cool my tongue. I am in anguish in this flame."

Abraham replied, "Son, in your earthly life, you enjoyed many good things but Lazarus knew only trouble and suffering. But now he knows comfort, and you are tormented. Plus, between us and you is a great division. We cannot come over to you, and you cannot cross over to us."

Then the rich man said, "Please, Father, send Lazarus to my family; I have five brothers. Let Lazarus warn them so that they don't have to come to this terrible place."

Abraham answered, "They have God's Word. It has the message of repentance and salvation."

"No, Father Abraham; if someone comes to them from the dead, they will repent."

But Abraham concluded, "If they won't listen to the Word of God, neither will they be convinced by someone who has risen from the dead."

Sheep or Goats? / Daniel 12:2

Look at the list below. Can you tell which lines describe sheep and which describe goats? Go through the list and guess *sheep*, *goats*, or *both* for each description.

- Gives us wool.
- Climbs on things.
- Has babies called lambs.
- Has babies called kids.
- Says "Baaaa."

You may not be sure about some of your answers. But if you had pictures, or if these animals were standing right in front of you, you'd have no doubt which were goats and which were sheep. The difference would be clear.

Daniel 12:2 talks about the day when Jesus will return to take us to heaven. Some people will have everlasting life and some will have everlasting death. Similarly, Matthew 25:31–33 talks about how God will separate believers and nonbelievers on the Last Day. All nations will be gathered before Him, and He will separate the "sheep" (people who believe in Jesus) from the "goats" (people who do not believe in Jesus). That sounds like quite a job!

So, how will Jesus be able to pick you and the rest of His sheep out of the great crowd on the Last Day? It's simple.

When He looks at you, He will see your faith in Him. He will see you, His forgiven child, the one He chose before the creation of the world and called by name.

Then Jesus will take you and all other believers to Himself to celebrate with Him forever and ever. You are and always will be a sheep of the Good Shepherd.

Talk about it: On the Last Day, those who believe in Jesus will go to heaven, but nonbelievers will go to hell. In what ways can you help nonbelievers to know Jesus?

Prayer: Thank You, dear Shepherd, that You call me by name. I am so blessed. Please use me to bring others to believe in You so that more people will go to heaven when they die. Praise be to You forever. Amen.

Let each of you look not only to his own interests, but also to the interests of others. Philippians 2:4

Jesus Meets Zacchaeus | Luke 19:1–9

Zacchaeus climbed up into a tree so he would be able to see Jesus as He came into town. Imagine his joy when Jesus invited Himself to stay with Zacchaeus, not only at Zacchaeus's house but, in another more important way, as Zacchaeus's Savior and friend through each day of his life. Zacchaeus was surprised, because he was a tax collector.

Tax collectors were looked down upon by others because they often became wealthy by collecting more from people than was due. And, as tax collectors go, Zacchaeus was rich. But when Jesus came into his life, Zacchaeus rejoiced in his Savior. His riches seemed of little value to him now. Zacchaeus now sought to serve God by sharing his wealth with others. Zacchaeus was sorry about the wrong things he had done. Jesus forgave Zacchaeus. Zacchaeus's heart changed. He told Jesus he would help poor people. He also said, "If I have cheated anybody out of anything, I will pay back four times the amount."

Honesty / Ephesians 4:28

Maria was usually cheerful and talkative, but she had been very quiet during dinner. Later, Maria was studying in her room when her mother peeked in.

"Hi, honey. What's goin' on?"

"Mom, have you ever cheated at anything?" Maria looked down at her history book.

Hesitating, Mrs. Vasquez said, "I remember once at the grocery store, the cashier gave me too much change. I didn't tell him. I prayed about it. After I talked with God, I returned the money."

"Some kids asked me to cheat on the history text tomorrow," Maria explained. "I know it's wrong to cheat, but I want to ace that test. I'm not sure just a prayer will help me do what's right."

Maria had a tough decision to make. She wasn't sure she could get an A without cheating. But she also knew that cheating is stealing and that it is wrong. She studied hard and prayed for God's strength and guidance.

Maria thought of Jesus. If she would cheat, it would be a sin. And Jesus suffered and died to pay for each of our sins.

The next morning, Maria had made her choice.

Talk about it: What do you think Maria did? What consequences may have followed if Maria decided to cheat? In what ways are cheating and stealing alike? How can you find help when you're tempted to do what you know is wrong?

Prayer: Lord Jesus, forgive me for the times I have sinned against You. Help me be the person You want me to be. Give me Your own strength so that I may live honestly and not take for myself anything I did not rightly earn. Thank You, Lord. Amen.

[Jesus said,] "I am the resurrection and the life. Whoever believes in Me, though he die, yet shall he live, and everyone who lives and believes in Me shall never die. John 11:25–26

Jesus Raises Lazarus from the Dead | John 11:1–44

Jesus had many friends. Some of His best friends were named Mary, Martha, and Lazarus. They lived in Bethany. Jesus often visited with them in their home. Now, Jesus was in another city. He heard that Lazarus was sick. Jesus did not hurry to see His old friend. He waited two days. Jesus knew that Lazarus had died. He planned to help Lazarus anyway.

At last, Jesus went to Bethany. Martha came to meet Jesus. They stood on the road and talked. Martha said, "If You had been here, my brother would not have died." Jesus said, "Lazarus will live again!" Soon, Mary came out to Jesus, along with some friends. She was very sad because Lazarus had died. Jesus was sad too. He cried.

Jesus and the people went to the place where Lazarus was buried. It was called a tomb. The tomb was a cave. A stone covered the entrance. Lazarus had been in the tomb for four days. The people were surprised when Jesus said, "Open the tomb." Some men took away the stone. Jesus shouted, "Lazarus, come out!" Lazarus walked out of the tomb. Jesus had made Lazarus alive again!

Someday, after we die, Jesus will bring us back to life, just as He restored life to Lazarus. But after He brings us back to life, Jesus will take us to live with Him in the happiness and joy of heaven. God promises in His Word that nothing can ever separate us from God and His love for us. Nothing . . . not even death.

Afraid of Falling Away / Psalm 23

Right now, you probably feel you love Jesus so much your heart could burst," Mr. Keiser told his Sunday School class. "As you grow older, it may get harder to stay close to Jesus. When you go to high school, some of your friends might make fun of you for being a Christian."

Candice started to worry. She did love Jesus a lot. But what if something happened when she got older? What if she forgot about Jesus? What if she stopped believing in Him? Then she wouldn't be able to go to heaven.

The next Sunday, Candice sat in church with her family and looked at the service folder. There was a picture of some lambs on the front. Candice looked at the picture while Pastor Young read the day's reading from the Bible. He read, "My sheep hear My voice, and I know them, and they follow Me. I give them eternal life, and they will never perish, and no one will snatch them out of My hand" (John 10:27–28).

When Candice was very young, she liked to sing "I am Jesus' Little Lamb." She pretended Jesus was holding her in His arms. Suddenly, Candice realized what Jesus' words in the Bible reading meant. In Baptism, Candice became a child of God. She was Jesus' little lamb, and He was holding her. She didn't have to be afraid about forgetting Jesus. He would never let her go. That is how Candice can be sure she will go to heaven.

Have you ever worried about falling away from the Savior? You don't need to worry. Jesus loves you so much that He gave His own life for you. He promises to take you to heaven. He's holding you right now, and He will never let you go. Not even death will separate us from God and His love for us in Jesus.

Psalm 23 is sometimes called the "Good Shepherd Psalm." The words of this psalm remind us "Even though I walk through the valley of the shadow of death, I will fear no evil, for You are with me; Your rod and Your staff, they comfort me" (v. 4).

When we have worry or doubt, we can remember Jesus and His love for us. He loved us so much He died to save us. And He has defeated death for us. He'll hold us close to Himself, for we are His lambs. He'll stay by our side, even through death itself. God has promised us in His Word that nothing can separate us from His love.

Talk about it: What worries or concerns do you have when you think about your faith in Jesus today? How can God's promises help you face and overcome these worries or concerns? Read Romans 8:38–39.

Prayer: Thank You, Jesus, for promising to keep us close to You always. Help us to live each day as Your people, trusting that we belong to You! Amen.

The Lord has established His throne in the heavens, and His kingdom rules over all. Psalm 103:19

Jesus Enters Jerusalem— Hosanna to the King!

Matthew 21:1–11

Just a few days before Jesus was to suffer and die for the sins of the world, something very special happened. Jesus rode into the city of Jerusalem on a donkey. The people welcomed Jesus into their city. Honoring Jesus as their king, many people placed their cloaks before Him on the road. Still others cut branches from the trees and spread them on the road. As Jesus passed by, the people shouted words of praise: "Hosanna to the Son of David! Blessed is He who comes in the name of the Lord." The children shouted just like the grown-ups, "Hosanna to the Son of David!"

Honoring Jesus in this way as a king fulfilled what a prophet had described many years before. He had written, "Behold, your king is coming to you, humble, and mounted on a donkey, and on a colt, the foal of a beast of burden." Jesus is indeed our king. As His followers, we are members of His kingdom.

The Kingdom of God / John 3:5

It's not fair," Greta wailed. "The boys keep calling themselves 'Kings of the Elm.' If I want to play in their tree house, I have to be ten years old, five feet tall, and a *boy*!"

"Why don't you help me wash the car? You can be Queen of the Chrome," suggested Mom. "Or you can help Dad cook dinner and be Princess of the Pots."

"But I want to be part of a *special* kingdom!" Greta huffed before sitting on the steps to the front porch.

"Oh, you are, Greta," Mom said, crouching beside her daughter. "Do you remember the part of the Lord's Prayer that talks about God's kingdom?"

"Thy kingdom come. That's what I want!" shouted Greta.

"But you are already part of the kingdom of God," said Mom, "You entered that kingdom when you were baptized in the name of the Father and of the Son and of the Holy Spirit. The pastor put water on you, and you were forever transformed."

"Transformed? I don't feel any different."

"In Baptism, the Holy Spirit worked faith in your heart. You became part of God's kingdom of grace. Baptism changes you so much that Jesus calls it being born again. You didn't look any different when you got baptized, but you became an heir of heaven."

"Are the boys part of this kingdom?" asked Greta.

"Yes, the boys were baptized too." Mom patted Greta on the back. "We love them too much to leave them out. Someday, Jesus will come again and take all of His children to live with Him in the kingdom of heaven."

"Like a prince coming to save his subjects?" asked Greta.

"Something like that. One thing's for sure—it will be the best day ever; the end of all your disappointments and the beginning of pure joy."

When we pray the Lord's Prayer and say, "Thy kingdom come," we ask that God give us the Holy Spirit. We also ask that God use us to bring others to His kingdom of grace so that more people will be prepared when Christ comes again in all His glory.

God's kingdom is truly a powerful, special place because it is filled with God's love!

Talk about it: God is an eternal, generous King. What gifts has He poured out on you?

Prayer: Dear Lord, may Your Word be preached everywhere so the kingdom of God may come to those who are still outside of it. Help us to live our lives for You. In Jesus' name we pray. Amen.

You shall love the Lord your God with all your heart and with all your soul and with all your mind. This is the great and first commandment. And a second is like it: You shall love your neighbor as yourself. Matthew 22:37–39

Jesus Teaches on the Ten Commandments

Matthew 22:34–39; Luke 10:25–37

Many years after God gave the Ten Commandments to His people, God sent His Son to earn forgiveness for every commandment we break because of our sinfulness and also to keep every commandment in our place.

Once, a man asked Jesus which of the commandments was the greatest. Jesus gave an excellent answer to the man's question. He summarized both parts of the Ten Commandments. He said the greatest commandment is to love God with all you are and have and to love your neighbor as yourself. The commandments are all about love.

Another time, Jesus told a story about love. In the story, a man was attacked by robbers. The robbers left the man wounded and almost dead. After two travelers passed by without stopping to help, a man who was from an enemy country saw the wounded man and helped him. He showed the man the kind of love Jesus showed to each of us when He lived and died in our place to save us.

Notice the Signs / Romans 13:8

Why are there so many different kinds of signs along this highway?" wondered Michael as he and his dad passed a flashing roadside message.

"Because drivers need a lot of information to drive carefully and reach their destinations safely," answered Dad. "The signs guide traffic and alert drivers of changes in the road—like that orange sign."

After a minute, Dad said, "I have an idea. To pass the time, let's look for all the different kinds of road signs. We can see how they help us drive safely and show love to other drivers."

"Show love to other drivers?" Michael giggled at the thought.

Dad wasn't surprised that Michael laughed. He explained that the kind of love that God wants us to have for one another is a helpful love; it doesn't harm. And a way to show that kind of love to others is to follow the road signs. So Michael and his dad noticed the signs—speed limits, mergers, no passing zones, and exits.

God's road signs of love are His Ten Commandments. The first three Commandments tell us how to love God. Matthew 22:37 sums up those first three Commandments: "Love the Lord your God with all your heart and with all your soul and with all your mind." The rest of the Commandments tell us how to love others. Matthew 22:39 says, "You shall love your neighbor as yourself." Did you notice that the word *love* is present in both of these verses? All of the Commandments can be summed up with that one word: *love*. Romans 13:10 says, "Love does no wrong to a neighbor; therefore love is the fulfilling of the law." God requires us humans to keep all His laws, but our sinful nature and sinful acts make that impossible for us. What was impossible for us was possible for Jesus. He fulfilled the Law. In doing so, He gave us a new sign—the cross—to remind us of His perfect victory over sin, death, and the devil. Jesus' resurrection is God's sign that one day we will be with Him in heaven.

Talk about it: Talk about the ways you can show love to either God or another person.

Prayer: Dear Jesus, thank You for being God's sign of love, my Savior. Help me to follow You. Amen.

The First Lord's Supper | Matthew 26:17–29

On the night before Jesus died on the cross to save us, He gathered His disciples around Him for a special meal. This special meal was the Passover meal. It celebrated the time when the people of Israel were living as slaves in Egypt. God had His people put blood from a lamb on the entrances to their homes. The angel passed over the homes on which the blood of the lamb had been spread and saved all those inside.

Jesus is the new Passover lamb. And as Jesus ate with His disciples that night, He began a new type of Passover meal. We call it the Lord's Supper. When Jesus gave the disciples bread that He had broken, He said, "Take, eat; this is My body." When He gave them wine to drink, He said, "Drink of it, all of you, for this is My blood." Jesus told the disciples to celebrate His special meal and remember His great love for them—a love that moved Jesus to suffer and die on the cross; a love that brings forgiveness of sins.

Participation Is Celebration / 1 Corinthians 10:15–17

Ms. Krause's students came from different churches, but they were all curious about the Lord's Supper.

A few weeks earlier, the question in "Q-Time" was "What is Communion like?" Ms. Krause decided to put off giving the answer until the students had time to interview three people and find out what Holy Communion was like for them.

That was a few weeks ago. She said they would discuss the question sometime soon after there had been a worship service with Communion. Today was the day.

Noel said he could always smell the wine on his dad's breath after he came back to the pew. When Andrew asked his grandma what it means, she said Communion made her certain that all her sins were forgiven, and it filled her with joy, hope, love, and peace. Alia asked Pastor Krume about it, and he said he always felt humble giving and receiving Jesus' own body and blood, participating with Jesus and others in such a sacred meal.

Ms. Krause said it is sort of like filling up your car with gas. When we become weak, Jesus' own body and blood make us strong. She also said it is like the gas used in furnaces and cooking stoves. She explained that natural gas doesn't have any odor, but the gas companies make it smell like rotten eggs so people know it is there. In the Lord's Supper, we can't see Jesus' body and blood, but in the bread and wine, we know it is there—because Jesus said so.

Forgiveness is ours all the time, but sometimes we might forget it or doubt it. Communion lets us smell, taste, and even touch our forgiveness in Jesus' own body and blood as we receive it in, with, and under the bread and the wine, so we know it is there. God prepares us to receive it in faith; we rejoice in the gift. It is a mystery, a miracle, and a marvelous gift!

Talk about it: Interview three people to find out what Holy Communion means to them.

Prayer: Dear God, thank You for assuring us of our forgiveness in Holy Communion. We thank You in Jesus' name. Amen.

See what kind of love the Father
has given to us,
that we should be called children
of God; and so we are. 1 John 3:1

Jesus Prays in the Garden | Matthew 26:30–46

After Jesus had shared the Last Supper with His disciples, He went with them into a garden called Gethsemane. He took Peter, James, and John aside with Him. Jesus began to be very troubled. He said, "My soul is overwhelmed with sadness to the point of death; stay here and keep watch with Me." He went away from them about as far as you can throw a stone and fell to the ground.

Jesus knew that suffering and pain would soon be upon Him, and He was greatly troubled because of it. Jesus talked to His Father in heaven. He prayed, "Father, all things are possible with You. Could You take away the suffering I will have to go through? Yet, let Your will be done."

Returning to Peter, James, and John, He found them asleep. Jesus said, "Watch and pray that you will not fall into temptation; the spirit is willing, but the body is weak."

Jesus went away a second time to pray. When He returned, He found them asleep again. A third time, Jesus went away to pray, saying the same words. Then an angel came from heaven to strengthen Jesus.

Jesus had received the answer to His prayer. His heavenly Father knew what would be best. Jesus knew the suffering, pain, and torment He would have to endure to save us. Willingly, Jesus walked into the dark night. He woke up the sleeping disciples. They arose to meet the soldiers who had come to arrest Jesus.

My Father Knows the Way / 1 Peter 5:7

Father was familiar with the city, but Ronald and his mother were not. Father, after all, had grown up in this city. Still, Ronald and his mother wondered about the way Father was taking them to get from the airport to Grandma's house. They seemed to be going in circles. Father drove them in their rental car down several dark alleys and through a very smoky industrial area.

"I think we just passed that same tree five minutes ago," whispered Ronald. "Dad, are you sure you know where you are going?"

Ronald's mother looked doubtfully out the window as they drove through an empty parking lot. Finally, she asked, "Wouldn't the highway have been a better option?"

Father replied, "This is the best way. Trust me."

Sure enough, the car pulled up to Grandma's house much earlier than they expected. Father really did know the best way.

Do you ever wonder if God really knows the best way to lead you in life? Sometimes, we spend time worrying about silly things like not having the right clothes to fit in at school or not getting the new bicycle we wanted for our birthday.

We sometimes worry about more serious things too, like whether our family will have enough money to pay the bills or repair damage to our home after a bad storm.

Just as Ronald and his mother doubted Father, we often doubt whether our heavenly Father will take care of our needs. We want control; we feel as though only we know what's best for our lives.

But we don't know. God alone knows what is best.

God created us, takes care of us, and knows the best way to take each of us through our lives. When life takes unexpected turns, we can rest assured that God has a plan.

He wants us to be saved so that we can spend eternity with Him. That's why He sent Jesus to be our Savior. Like a loving father, God promises to be with us through joyful times and scary times, sad and lonely times too.

We can count on our Father in heaven to hear our every prayer. He has promised to do so for Jesus' sake. Even though God doesn't always give us what we *want*, we can count on God to give us all we *need*. He always knows the best way.

Talk about it: What blessings has God given your family? When has God worked things out for good in your life?

Prayer: *Heavenly Father, thank You for sending Jesus to be my Savior. Help me to trust in the way You care for all my needs. Help me to talk to You regularly and often in prayer. Help me to trust in You and in Your love and care for me. In Jesus' name I pray. Amen.*

If You, O LORD, should mark iniquities,
O Lord, who could stand?
But with You there is forgiveness,
that You may be feared.
Psalm 130:3–4

Jesus Earns Our Forgiveness | Matthew 27:27–56; Luke 23:32–49; John 19:1–30

After Jesus was arrested, Pontius Pilate, the Roman governor, put a crown of thorns and a purple robe on Jesus to mock Him and make Him suffer. Then Pilate gave in to the people and sentenced Jesus to death. Soldiers led Jesus to Golgotha (Calvary). Here, at nine o'clock in the morning, they nailed Jesus to a cross.

Jesus' body suffered horrible pain. In addition, people taunted and humiliated Jesus. Soldiers mocked Him and gambled for His clothes. Offering Him sour wine, they said, "If You are the King of the Jews, save yourself." Above His head was posted a sign intended to ridicule Him.

Jesus' response? He prayed to His Father in heaven. Jesus prayed not for Himself but, rather, for His enemies. "Father, forgive them," Jesus said, "for they know not what they do."

Two thieves were crucified with Jesus. One asked Jesus to remember him in heaven. Jesus said, "Today you will be with Me in Paradise."

Then, looking down from the cross, Jesus saw His mother and the disciple John. Jesus said, "Dear woman, here is your son" and "Son, here is your mother." From that moment on, John took care of Mary as if she were his mother.

From noon until three o'clock, there was darkness over the land. At about three o'clock, Jesus cried out, "My God, My God, why have You forsaken Me?"

He said, "I thirst," and so they gave Him vinegar to drink. Then Jesus said, "It is finished. Father, into Your hands I commend My spirit," and died. A Roman centurion said, "Surely He was the Son of God!"

Forgiven and Forgetting / Matthew 6:14–15

Corrie ten Boom lived in Holland during World War II. Corrie and her family watched as Nazis rounded up Jewish families—mothers, fathers, children, grandparents—and sent them off to die of starvation, disease, and brutality in concentration camps.

Despite dangers, Corrie ten Boom and her family protected and hid Jewish people. When the Nazis found out, the ten Boom family was arrested.

Corrie's father was killed by Nazi soldiers, while Corrie and her sister were sent to a death camp. Corrie's sister Betsie died, but Corrie survived and eventually returned home.

After the war, Corrie spoke to groups of people about the horrors of prison camp. She told how Jesus was with her in that horrible place. She also talked about God's forgiveness.

At the end of one of her talks, Corrie began shaking hands with listeners. Suddenly, she felt cold all over. A former guard at the death camp stood before her with a smile on his face. He extended his hand to shake hers. "I'm so glad to know that Jesus forgives me," he said.

The image of the cruelty at the death camp flashed in Corrie's mind. She didn't want to shake the man's hand. She prayed for God to help her forgive the former prison guard.

Corrie remembered that God's love and forgiveness is for *all* people. Through Jesus Christ, God forgives all our sins.

The former prison guard repented and trusted in Jesus as his Savior. God forgave him. Corrie remembered that she is also a sinner who is continually forgiven through Christ Jesus.

With God's help, Corrie shook the man's hand and forgave him. By forgiving the former prison guard, Corrie showed that she truly believed in God's forgiveness. Through Jesus' death for your sins, God forgives you too. That love and forgiveness of God gives you the power to forgive others.

In the Lord's Prayer, we ask God to help us forgive the sins of others in the same way that God forgives us. After all, the Bible tells us, "Be kind to one another, tenderhearted, forgiving one another, as God in Christ forgave you" (Ephesians 4:32).

Talk about it: Is there someone whom you find hard to forgive? How can remembering that God forgives your sins help you forgive others?

Prayer: Dear God, I know that I need Your forgiveness. Thank You for sending Jesus to die for my sins and the sins of all people. Help me forgive others, just as You forgive me. In Jesus' name I pray. Amen.

The blood of Jesus His Son cleanses us from all sin. 1 John 1:7

Jesus Is Crucified to Save Us | Mark 15:6–39

Jesus had to die. People who hated Jesus said so. But God said so too. God loved His Son, Jesus. But He also loved us. Jesus died to take away our sins. Here is how it happened:

Jesus had done nothing wrong. Still, His enemies put Him on trial. Some people shouted, "Crucify Him! Crucify Him!" They wanted soldiers to nail Jesus to a cross. They wanted Jesus to hang from the cross until He died. Pilate, the Roman governor, said, "Take Jesus away and crucify Him."

They brought Jesus to a hill called Calvary (or Golgotha). They nailed Jesus' hands and feet to the cross. They lifted the cross and placed it into a hole in the ground. People passed by the cross.

Many of them made fun of Jesus. They didn't believe He was the Savior.

It was early afternoon, but the sky grew dark! Jesus hurt all over. He spoke from the cross. Then He died. There was a terrible earthquake. Big rocks split. The thick curtain in the temple tore from top to bottom. One of the Roman soldiers guarding the cross said, "Jesus really was the Son of God!"

We remember the day when Jesus died. We call it "Good Friday." We call it a "good" day even though it was so very sad because on Good Friday Jesus died for the sins of the world. He paid for our sins. Now we can be forgiven and live some day forever with God in heaven!

He Took Our Sins upon Himself / 2 Corinthians 5:21

"Class, it's time for Bible study," announced the teacher, Mrs. Reitz. "Today, we will need a volunteer to be Jesus."

Of course, all the students wanted to be Jesus, so they all raised their hands. Mrs. Reitz chose the most eager volunteer.

"Okay, Jason, come up here in front of the class. The rest of you may go to your lockers to get your coats."

The children returned wearing their fluffy, warm coats. They were also wearing confused looks on their faces.

"Now," Mrs. Reitz explained, "let's imagine that these are *sin coats*. When God sees you,

He sees that you're wearing a sin coat. So each of you, bring yours up here to Jesus. He will take them from you and put them on."

The children enjoyed the fun as Jason donned coat after coat. But it wasn't long before he began to wish he hadn't volunteered. He could hardly stand up under the weight of all the coats! He was also getting quite warm, and beads of sweat broke out on his forehead.

The teacher continued, "All of our sin coats are now on Jesus. He took them also from everyone who had ever lived and ever would live. He did this out of love for us."

Mrs. Reitz quietly let Jason crawl out from under the pile of coats. Then she continued, "When Jesus died, He took away our sins. They are gone! Now when God looks at us, He sees that Jesus has removed our sin coats. So, children, what have you learned today?"

Jason sighed and said, "I learned not to be so quick to volunteer to be Jesus!"

〜〜〜〜〜〜〜

Talk about it: How does it make you feel when someone helps you carry a heavy load? How does it make you feel that Jesus has removed your load of sins?

Prayer: Dear Jesus, Your great love is more than I can comprehend. Thank You for volunteering to take my sins and die for them in my place. Amen.

Jesus Is Risen! He Is Risen Indeed! | Matthew 28:1–15

The friends of Jesus were sad. They were afraid too. Jesus was dead. They thought Jesus' enemies might kill them. Jesus was buried in a place called a tomb. It was like a cave. The door to the cave was covered with a big rock. Soldiers guarded the tomb. They didn't want anyone to take Jesus' body.

It was Sunday morning. There was an earthquake. An angel came down from heaven and rolled away the big rock. The soldiers were so afraid that they fell over. Two of Jesus' friends came to His tomb. Both of them were named Mary. The two Marys could see inside the tomb. They were afraid. The angel said, "Don't be afraid. I know you are looking for Jesus. He isn't in the tomb. He came back to life, just as He said. You will see Him soon."

The two Marys were happy. They ran from the tomb. Suddenly, they stopped. They saw Jesus. He was alive! They ran to Him. Jesus said, "Go and tell My disciples that you saw Me. Tell them I am alive. I will meet them later."

We call this happy day "Easter." Easter is a day of celebration. On this day, we remember that Jesus once was dead but came back to life again. Christians down through the years have greeted one another in a special way on Easter Sunday. When people say, "He is risen!" others say back, "He is risen indeed!" Easter is a happy day because after we die, Jesus will bring us back from the dead, just as He brought Himself back from death to life.

What Death Is Like / 1 Thessalonians 4:16

When Gretchen was growing up, her parents hardly ever hired a babysitter. When her mom and dad visited friends in the evening, they brought Gretchen along with them. And the other parents brought their kids too. Gretchen and her friends would pile their families' coats in a mountain on the bed and then get down to business. While the adults talked, the children played and played . . . and then played some more.

One night, the kids got tired and lay across the coat-covered bed. Gretchen and her sister snuggled in and fell asleep.

When they woke up, they weren't even near the pile of coats. They were in their own beds. They were wearing pajamas. It seemed as though one moment they were one place, and the next they were home.

While Gretchen and her sister were asleep, their parents did all the work. They carried them from the bed to the car and from the car to their own beds. They switched their play clothes for sleepwear. They prayed over them instead of with them.

When we die, God does the same thing for us. That's what it means when we say, "I believe in the resurrection of the body."

One second, we will fall asleep on earth, and the next we will be home in heaven. The Bible also tells us that on the Last Day, Christ will come again and take us to live with Him in glory. Jesus does all the work. He died on the cross for our sins, He arose on Easter, and He ascended back to heaven to prepare a place for us. When our time on earth is over, we will fall asleep in Jesus. He will take His children home to be with Him forever.

Talk about it: How can we be sure that when we die we will wake up in heaven?

Prayer: Dear Jesus, thank You for saving me through Your death and resurrection so that I will go to heaven when I die. Give me guidance and power to live, knowing that I am always in Your loving arms. Amen.

I have been crucified with Christ. It is no longer I who live, but Christ who lives in me. And the life I now live in the flesh I live by faith in the Son of God, who loved me and gave Himself for me. Galatians 2:20

Jesus Teaches Thomas | Luke 24:36–48; John 20:24–29

It was the evening of the first Easter day. The disciples had locked themselves inside a house. They were afraid that the same people who killed Jesus might want to kill them. They also heard from friends who said that Jesus was alive. They were mixed up, and they didn't know what to do.

The disciples talked about all that had happened. Suddenly, Jesus was standing in the room with them! The disciples thought He was a ghost. They were afraid.

Jesus said, "Why are you afraid? Why don't you believe that I am alive?" Jesus told the disciples to touch Him. He showed them the nail holes in His hands and feet. Then He asked for something to eat. Now they knew that Jesus wasn't a ghost. Ghosts don't have bodies. Ghosts can't eat! The disciples knew that Jesus was alive.

The disciple named Thomas wasn't with them that night. Later, when the other disciples told him they had seen Jesus, Thomas didn't believe them. He wanted to see for himself. So Jesus appeared again the next week. He told Thomas, "Put your finger here; see My hands. Stop doubting and believe." Thomas's heart changed. He said, "My Lord and my God!" Now He believed that Jesus was alive. Jesus blesses us today for believing this truth even though we have not seen Him.

Name above All Names / Philippians 2:9–11

Hey, Zip!" That's what Andrew used to hear when he was growing up. He was a skinny kid. One day, Andrew's brother told him that if he stood sideways and stuck out his tongue, someone would mistake him for a zipper. Unfortunately, some of Andrew's friends heard him say that, and so he got Zip for a nickname.

A nickname usually tells something about a person. Sometimes it's a compliment, but sometimes it isn't.

As time passed, Andrew grew up and changed, and the nickname Zip no longer applied. You might say Andrew outgrew it.

The Bible gives many names for Jesus. One of these names is Christ. The name Christ means "Messiah." It reminds us that Jesus is the Savior promised to be born among God's people. This name and all other names for Jesus tell us something about Jesus as a person and about His life and work for us.

All of these names apply. They always will, because Jesus will never outgrow them.

Philippians 2:9–11 reminds us that the name of Jesus is above all other names and that one day all people will kneel before Him and honor Him as Lord. Jesus' name is the greatest of all names because Jesus is the only Savior of the world.

Talk about it: Jesus has many names. Each name reminds us of something about Jesus. What is your favorite name for Jesus? Why?

Prayer: So many wonderful names apply to you, dear Jesus! Thank You that You are my Savior and Lord. Amen.

Do you not know that you are God's temple and that
God's Spirit dwells in you? 1 Corinthians 3:16

The Holy Spirit Comes at Pentecost | Acts 2

God the Father is God; Jesus is God; and the Holy Spirit is God. God is triune—three in one—the Trinity—one true God. The Holy Spirit came in a powerful way to God's people at Pentecost, just ten days after Jesus, in His body, rose up into the air to go to heaven. Jesus had told His followers to go to Jerusalem and wait for the Spirit.

When the Holy Spirit came, Jesus' followers heard a strong wind and saw what looked like flames hovering over their heads. What happened next was even more surprising. They began speaking in different languages. They had not learned to speak those languages, but now they could speak them because of a miracle of God. People from other countries could understand what they were saying. Now Jesus' followers could tell everyone about Jesus!

A crowd of people gathered outside the house. Peter spoke to them about Jesus, our Lord and Savior. Many people believed Peter. About three thousand people were baptized that day. That special day was called Pentecost. The people continued each day to worship God and learn more about forgiveness and salvation.

The work of the Holy Spirit is giving people faith. The Holy Spirit works faith through God's Word as it is read or heard or received in Baptism or the Lord's Supper. The Holy Spirit also brings people together, uniting them in one large and powerful group, known as the Church.

The Work of the Holy Spirit / Acts 2:1–4

Many people enjoy watching the Olympic Games. The games alternate from a winter to a summer version. Several months before the opening ceremony of the Olympics, a torch is lit. It is always lit in Athens, Greece, where the Olympics began, using the sun's rays and a mirror.

From one to another, athletes pass the torch, carrying it throughout the continents. Finally, on the day of the opening ceremony, the torch enters the Olympic stadium. With this signal, the games begin.

The torch represents the unity and the peace of the Olympic Games. It is a visual way of showing that, at least for a few weeks, the competing countries unite for a common purpose.

Pentecost is a special day in the life of the Christian Church. In fact, it is the beginning of the Christian Church. On Pentecost, we thank God that He sent the Holy Spirit to His Church.

On that first Pentecost, the followers of Jesus gathered in Jerusalem. Suddenly, they heard a sound like a strong wind. The sound filled the whole house. Tongues of fire came to rest on each of them. The Holy Spirit filled them, and they began to speak about Jesus in other languages.

Although the Olympic torch represents unity and peace among the nations involved, that peace and unity do not last. Disputes break out, and arguments arise. Family and friends, neighborhoods and cities don't have peace, either.

On Pentecost, when God's Spirit arrived, the message of what Jesus had done on Calvary's cross brought true unity and peace. The Holy Spirit makes people holy and brings them to faith in Christ. The Holy Spirit brings God's peace because by nature we are enemies of God. We can trust, rejoice, and find comfort in Him—the one who brings unity and peace.

Talk about it: When did the Holy Spirit bring you to faith in Jesus?

Prayer: Holy Spirit, thank You for making me holy by bringing me to faith in Christ so that I might be saved. In Jesus' name I pray. Amen.

Philip and the Ethiopian | Acts 8:26–40

Philip was a special helper in the Church. One day, an angel told Philip to start walking down a road through the desert. Philip walked and walked. A man riding in a chariot went by. He was reading from the Bible. The man was from Africa. He worked for the queen of Ethiopia.

The Holy Spirit told Philip to catch up with the chariot. Philip ran and ran. He came alongside the chariot. Philip asked, "Do you understand what you are reading?" The man said, "I'm reading from the Bible book written by Isaiah. I don't understand it at all. Can you tell me what it means?"

Philip had Good News for the man. He said, "The words of the prophet Isaiah have been fulfilled by Jesus Christ. Jesus died to take your sins away. Then He rose from the dead. Now He lives in heaven. Jesus did all this to take away our sins and to give us the promise of eternal life."

The man believed. He asked Philip to baptize him. They stopped by some water. Philip baptized the man from Africa. Then the man climbed into his chariot. He went on his way rejoicing. He wanted to go home and tell everyone the Good News. The Holy Spirit took Philip to another place to tell people there about Jesus.

This story tells us about the work of God's Spirit. God's Spirit brings people to faith in Jesus through the Word. He welcomes us into God's kingdom through Baptism. And He brings us the joy of knowing that Christ Jesus has saved us.

This story also tells us about good works. Good works are the things God's people do because God's Spirit is at work in them. When Philip told the Ethiopian about Jesus, he was doing a good work. But there are many other types of good works as well. Whenever God's Spirit helps us serve God and others, He helps us to do a good work as forgiven and redeemed people of God.

Good Works by the Holy Spirit / John 15:5

Albert lived an unusual life. By the time he was thirty, Albert had already written three books and become a pastor. Later, he became a professor and was known throughout the world as a talented organist and music scholar.

But Albert was troubled. While he excelled in music and enjoyed studying and teaching God's word in Europe, he learned that people in Africa were suffering from disease and starvation. Albert's heart ached when he thought about the pain and hardships of the African people. He longed to help. The world-famous teacher and musician decided to become a doctor. After studying medicine, Albert and his wife moved to Africa to build a hospital.

Some people called Albert Schweitzer foolish. A man with so many talents, they said, should not hide away in a far-off land. Just think how wealthy he would be if he stayed in Europe!

Albert had a different idea. He kept writing books and taking trips abroad. Albert continued to work with people in Africa; he believed that God wanted him to take care of others.

We don't all have to become doctors and move to Africa in order to please God. A good work in God's sight is anything that a person does, speaks, or thinks to the glory of God or to benefit another person.

As sinners, though, we can't possibly do good works on our own. The Holy Spirit creates faith within us, and through that faith He renews our life so that we strive to do good. Albert was moved by the Holy Spirit to help ease the suffering in Africa; each of us are moved by the Holy Spirit when we help others. Apart from the Holy Spirit, humans can do no good.

Although good works please God, they certainly are not enough to get us to heaven. Thankfully, Jesus gave up His life for us on the cross. In Baptism, we receive God's forgiveness, salvation, and the Holy Spirit. As God's forgiven and free children, we can use our gifts to glorify God and to help other people. The Holy Spirit gives us the ability to live as God's children.

Talk about it: What special talents has God given you that you can use to glorify God or help others?

Prayer: Thank You, heavenly Father, for making us Your children through Baptism. Thank You for Your Holy Spirit and the good works He moves us to do. We praise You in Jesus' name. Amen.

For I am not ashamed of the gospel, for it is the power of God for salvation to everyone who believes, to the Jew first and also to the Greek. Romans 1:16

Jesus Changes Saul (aka Paul) | Acts 9:1–28

After the coming of the Holy Spirit at Pentecost, the early Christian Church began to grow rapidly. But there were also people who opposed the Christians. Saul, an enemy of the followers of Jesus, was authorized to find and arrest Christians in Damascus.

As he traveled to that city, suddenly a bright light from heaven shined on him. Falling to the ground, Saul heard a voice say, "Saul, Saul, why are you persecuting Me?"

Saul asked, "Who are You, Lord?"

And the Lord said, "I am Jesus, whom you are persecuting." Jesus told Saul to go to the city, where he would be told what to do. When Saul got up, he was unable to see. Those who were with him had to lead him into the city.

Meanwhile, Jesus spoke to a disciple named Ananias, who lived in Damascus. He told Ananias to go to Saul and help him. Ananias didn't want to go. He had heard that Saul hated Christians. Jesus said, "Go. Saul will tell many people about Me." So Ananias went with a message from Jesus. Saul's sight was restored, and he was baptized.

Then Saul began to preach the Good News of Jesus in Damascus. Now his former friends were his enemies. They were angry that he had changed. They wanted to capture him. So his new Christian friends let Saul down over the wall of the city in a basket to escape. Saul, also known as Paul, went to Jerusalem and spoke boldly of the Lord Jesus.

Jesus changed Paul. Paul was once a man who hated those who believed in Jesus. Now, he was a missionary. As a missionary, Paul would tell people all over the world the Good News about Jesus. The Good News about Jesus is called the Gospel. Writing to believers in the city of Rome, Paul talked about the Gospel. The Gospel tells us that Jesus lived, died, and rose again to earn forgiveness of sins and home in heaven for all people.

Paul writes, "I am not ashamed of the gospel, for it is the power of God for salvation to everyone who believes." The power of the Gospel brings people to faith. The power of the Gospel takes away our sins, even as it gives us the power to also forgive those who sin against us.

Hallway Trouble / 2 Corinthians 5:17

Rebecca's first day of school meant that she could finally wear her new purple shirt! She liked it because the words "Jesus Is Lord" were written across the front and the bright color made Rebecca smile—purple was her favorite. It looked great with her new jeans too. Rebecca was very excited for her first day!

As Rebecca walked through the door of her classroom, she saw her least-favorite person—Jennifer. She was standing with some other girls and giggled when she saw Rebecca. "Look at Becca. Thinks she's so cool with her bad hair and no-name jeans," said Jennifer.

Rebecca's cheeks burned hot, and she ran down the hall. She was in such a hurry that she ran right into Jason. Her books slipped from her arms and slammed to the ground.

"I heard Jennifer," Jason said, picking up her books. "That was really rotten of her. Want me to help you get even?"

Rebecca wiped her eyes and thought: *Get even! Oh, yes! Wouldn't it be great to get back at Jennifer with one of Jason's pranks?* But she knew it wasn't right.

"No, I'll get over it," she said after a minute. "Let's just go to class."

God doesn't "get even" with us when we sin. Through Jesus Christ, God gives us forgiveness, faith, and life. We call this great news "the Gospel." Because Jesus died for our sins and gave us forgiveness, we are able to forgive others just as Rebecca forgave Jennifer. Because Rebecca gave Jennifer forgiveness, Jason saw God at work.

"Wow, you really do believe it!" Jason said.

"Believe what?" asked Rebecca.

"The words on your shirt."

"You're right," she said, smiling.

Talk about it: Read John 3:16 aloud. What is the good news that this verse talks about? Why is it important for us as sinners?

Prayer: Loving Father, thank You so much for the Gospel! Please give us patience and endurance when problems come so that we might reflect God's love. In Jesus' name we pray. Amen.

Do not be anxious about anything, but in everything by prayer and supplication with thanksgiving let your requests be made known to God. Philippians 4:6

Peter Freed from Prison | Acts 12:1–19

Peter was in danger. Wicked King Herod had put him in prison. Herod was about to send for him. Perhaps Peter's days on earth were coming to an end.

But the Christians prayed for Peter without stopping. God heard and answered their prayers. The night before Herod would have sent for him, Peter was tied in chains, sleeping between two soldiers. Guards stood before the door of the prison. Suddenly, an angel from the Lord came to Peter, shining a light on him, nudging him, and saying, "Get up quickly."

Peter's chains fell from his hands, and Peter followed the angel from the prison. At first, Peter thought he was seeing a vision. When they came to the iron gate leading to the city, it opened for them by itself. They were walking on a city street when suddenly the angel left Peter.

When Peter realized what had happened, he said, "Now I know for sure that the Lord has sent His angel to deliver me from the hand of Herod and from my enemies." Peter came to the house of Mary, the mother of John Mark, where many believers had gathered to pray. Peter's knock was answered by a young woman named Rhoda. When she heard Peter's voice, she was so overjoyed she forgot to open the door to let Peter in. Instead, she ran and told everyone that Peter stood outside the door.

Those inside refused to believe Rhoda, but she insisted that Peter was outside. Meanwhile, Peter continued to knock at the door. When they opened the door and saw him, they were amazed. Asking them to listen, Peter proceeded to tell the assembly how the Lord had answered their prayers. God had sent His angel and brought Peter out of prison. Peter said, "Go and tell these things to James and to the other brothers." Then Peter left.

This story reminds us that when we pray to God, God hears our prayers. And God answers them!

Expect an Answer / Acts 12:13–17

David had plans to build a hutch for Chester, his rabbit. But he couldn't do the project by himself. He needed his dad's help. David knew that his dad was a busy man, so he didn't really expect his dad to help, even though he had asked him to.

On his own, David got wood, tools, and carpentry plans. But the directions were hard to understand. Was he even holding the paper in the right direction? He was becoming more and more confused and frustrated. But then something unexpected happened. David's dad joined him! His dad had been planning to help David all along. Together, they built a beautiful hutch in no time.

Long ago, the apostle Peter had been thrown in jail, and King Herod was probably planning to put him to death. Peter's friends were gathered that night to pray for him. They spoke to God with their words and in their thoughts. While they prayed, something unexpected happened! An angel came and miraculously released Peter from jail.

When Peter joined his praying friends, they couldn't believe he was at the door. They even thought Rhoda, who heard him knock, was out of her mind! They really didn't expect God to answer their prayers.

Do we sometimes act as though we don't expect our heavenly Father to answer our prayers? Maybe we talk to God about something, but then we keep worrying as though we don't think God will help us. But God promises to hear our prayers for Jesus' sake. He promises to answer them in the time and way that are best for us. We can speak to God through prayer and expect an answer!

Talk about it: What are some things you can pray for every morning when you wake up?

Prayer: Dear heavenly Father, thank You for giving me a way to talk to You. Thank You for hearing my prayers. Help me to always expect an answer from You, trusting that You know what and when it's best for me. I pray in Jesus' name. Amen.

Lydia Comes to Faith | Acts 16:11–15

Paul and his friend Silas traveled to many distant countries, telling people the Good News of Jesus. Eventually, their travels took them to Philippi in the present-day country of Greece on the continent of Europe.

On the day when people got together to worship God, Paul and Silas went outside the city to the river. Here, they expected to find a place of prayer. They sat down and began to speak about Jesus to the women who had gathered there. One of those women was Lydia. She made a living dealing in purple cloth.

As Paul and Silas talked about Jesus, Lydia listened to what they were saying. The Holy Spirit used God's Word as it was spoken by Paul to change Lydia's heart. Lydia became a believer in Jesus! Lydia and the members of her family were baptized. And Lydia invited Paul and Silas to come and stay at her house.

New Fingerprints / 2 Corinthians 5:17

Something caught four-year-old Ryan's eye as he was drinking a glass of milk. "Mom, there are funny-looking marks on this glass."

"Those are your fingerprints," his mother said. "Look closely at them. You will see tiny little lines in them."

Scientists believe that of the billions of people in the world, no two people have the same fingerprints. Every one of our fingers has a unique print, and each of us has prints different than everyone else's prints.

There are three basic pattern groups in the fingerprint ridges. Most people have loops. There are also arch patterns and whorl patterns. What are you? What-

ever your fingerprint pattern, you are one of a kind.

We have an expert who can identify each of us even without using our fingerprints. That expert is our Creator, our God. He knows everything about each one of us. He knows we are sinners, and yet He loves us. He promised to save sinners, and He planned our salvation through the sacrifice of His own Son, Jesus.

Our creative God also planned a way for faith to come to us. Here is how it can happen: In Baptism, the Holy Spirit gives us faith. Through water and God's Word, this holy and divine event occurs. God the Holy Spirit creates a new

person—a child of God. When we confess our sins before God, He forgives us for Jesus' sake and helps us lead a new life in Him.

Each day, as we grow by the power of the Holy Spirit in true faith and good works, we can use our new-person fingers to leave behind new-person fingerprints. In Christ, we are a new creation! And that's reason for joy!

Talk about it: On a piece of paper, make a print of your finger. Beside it, write, "In Christ, I am a new creation." What does it mean to you that God has made you a new creation?

Prayer: Holy Spirit, You forgive my sins and make me new every single day. Guide me today in faith that I know true joy and do those things that show Your power in my life. I pray in Jesus' name, with thanks for all He has done for me. Amen.

For by grace you have been saved through faith. And this is not your own doing; it is the gift of God, not a result of works, so that no one may boast.   Ephesians 2:8–9

A Jailer Receives the Gospel | Acts 16:22–34

Saul, also called Paul, became a great missionary. He traveled to many places to preach the Gospel. Many people, however, did not want to hear the message about Jesus.

In Philippi, Paul and his helper Silas were arrested, beaten, and thrown into prison. Inside the prison, Paul and Silas sat with their feet locked in wooden stocks. Still, they were not discouraged. At midnight, while they were praying and singing hymns, an earthquake shook the foundations of the prison. The doors opened, and the chains that held Paul and Silas fell off.

The jailer awoke from sleep and, seeing the open prison doors, took out a sword to kill himself. Paul called out, "Do not harm yourself. We are all here." The jailer called for lights, rushed to Paul and Silas, and fell trembling before them. He said, "Sirs, what must I do to be saved?"

They replied, "Believe in the Lord Jesus Christ, and you will be saved." The jailer took Paul and Silas to his home and washed their wounds. He and his whole family were baptized. The jailer was filled with joy. And so the jailer and his whole family believed the Gospel and became Christians.

God's Grace Changes Things / Romans 3:23

When Ceandre first brought the desk home, his family couldn't believe he had actually paid money for it. The front of one drawer was halfway off, deep scratches covered the top, and the entire desk wobbled. Once his family stopped laughing at him, he said only two words: "Just wait." He repeated, "Just wait."

Ceandre went to work. He reattached the front of the drawer. He tightened and reglued every joint in the desk to make it sturdy. Then he stripped the dirty, scratched paint with a chemical remover and sanded the entire desk. Finally, he applied a wood stain and protective seal.

When his family saw the result of his work, they expressed amazement. The desk looked great and was sturdy enough to use every day. The family's two children even fought over who got to use it.

God works a somewhat similar change in us when He brings us to faith. We were once marred and dirty with sin, but Jesus bought us and paid for us with His blood. Then He changed us into new people. We refer to God's changing of us as the workings of His grace.

Ceandre's desk couldn't renew itself. Neither can we change ourselves by our own power. God makes us the people He wants us to be through the power of His Word. He gives us His Spirit to help us do His will.

With daily use, the refinished desk will weaken and become dirty again. And living in a sinful world and our own sin make us weak and dirty with sin. That's why we depend on God to wash away our sins. We trust in His grace. And we rejoice in the strength He gives us to do His will, living as His people. What God does for us through Jesus by His grace is truly a wonderful and awesome thing. It is the main message of the Bible!

Talk about it: What do you do when you find yourself weak and sinful? How can you thank Jesus for saving you?

Prayer: Dear Father, thank You for making me Your child and a new person through Jesus. Thank You for Your love and grace. Help me to share Your love with others. In Jesus' name I pray. Amen.

Paul Suffers Much for the Gospel

2 Corinthians 1:3–8; 6:1–5

Paul was a great missionary, perhaps the greatest all of time. He traveled all over the world to tell people the Good News of Jesus. But things weren't always easy for Paul. In fact, much of what he experienced could be called suffering or hardship. He was often in prison, was beaten severely, and even had enemies who once tried to kill him by throwing stones at him.

Three times, he was shipwrecked, and he spent many hours on the open sea. Often, he went without sleep or food or clothing. Paul might have focused on the things he didn't have but wanted in order to feel comfortable. Instead, though, he found contentment in Jesus and in the work he was doing.

Paul wanted to bring the Good News of Jesus' love and forgiveness to those who had not yet heard about it. Paul wanted to share it with others because of the change Jesus had made in his life.

Contentment / Psalm 145:9–13

It was too nice and warm to stay inside after school. Beth walked over to visit her neighbor Ann, who was sitting on her porch swing.

"I'm reading a diary," said Ann. "I found something I wrote years ago on this date."

"That's neat," said Beth. "What was it?"

"Come and sit down with me, and I'll read you what this says. 'Warm sun on the concrete step; a good talk with a favorite friend; mint tea and old-fashioned oatmeal cookies; robins along the fence; a butterfly on a dandelion; jonquils, magnolias, and tulips in bloom; green in the tree branches; a song in my mind.'

"I still remember the song I had on my mind when I wrote this," Ann explained. "It's the Johnny Appleseed song."

After Ann sang it to Beth, they sang it together while swinging. The sweet ending and beginning, "The Lord is good to me," fit that gorgeous April day.

The Lord fills our lives with blessings. All our happiness comes from Him. He gives us everything we need. Our greatest need is to be saved from sin and death. So our most important blessing is the forgiveness Jesus earned for us. Without that blessing, we couldn't really be happy, even if we had everything else we wanted.

Because of Jesus, every day is a wonderful day. It's another day to live for Him, even when there are no cookies baking or tulips blooming. We can know contentment even when things around us aren't all that wonderful. Because our Savior rose from the dead, we look forward to perfect happiness in heaven. And that's something to sing about!

Talk about it: Write about good things God puts into your life. Save what you write and look at it next year.

Prayer: Thank You, Lord, for all the beauties and pleasures of life. You are so good to me. Amen.

[God] desires all people to be saved and to come to the knowledge of the truth.
1 Timothy 2:4

Paul Serves God as a Missionary | Romans 8:28

Sometime after Paul's third missionary trip, he was arrested and taken to Rome to stand trial as a Roman citizen. While sailing to Italy, his ship faced a terrible storm. The wind raged, and the waves splashed.

Neither the sun nor the stars could be seen for many days. The people began to give up hope of being saved. Paul encouraged them by telling of a message God had given him through an angel. God's message said that though their ship would be destroyed, not one of them would die.

When they were shipwrecked, Paul and his fellow travelers swam or floated to the nearby island of Malta. The friendly island people of Malta built a fire to warm the cold and wet newcomers. When Paul threw sticks onto the fire, a poisonous snake bit him.

Paul shook the snake into the fire. Paul suffered no harm because God had said he would live to reach Rome. From Malta, Paul and his shipmates traveled on safely to Rome. Paul was greeted in Rome by the Christians there, who were glad to see him. For two years, Paul remained in Rome under house arrest, preaching the Good News of Jesus, the Son of God and Savior of the world.

Each of these things that happened in Paul's life was part of God's plan for him. God planned for Paul, once a persecutor of God's people, to become a great missionary who would take the Good News into all the world. And so Paul did. It was God's will, part of His plan. And God's will for each of us is that we come to faith in Jesus and live our lives for Him.

First Things First / Acts 9:1–16

Do you have a baby book? If so, it probably records your famous firsts: your first tooth, your first steps, your first words, and your first day of school. What were some of your first achievements? Perhaps you worked hard at learning to read, at hitting a baseball, or at using a computer program.

The word *first* means "before any others" or "most important." What comes first for you? Getting good grades? Being an excellent athlete, actor, or piano player?

Setting goals and working to achieve them is wise, as long as you do something else first.

The birth of the Church was at Pentecost; after that, the Church endured a time of persecution. Chief among those who hunted down and punished Jesus' followers was a man named Saul (Paul). Paul thought he was serving God with his attempts to squelch the growing Church, but Paul was really serving the devil. Jesus intervened. He met Paul on the road to Damascus and, for Paul and the Christian Church, things were never the same again. Jesus changed Paul, and Paul became a follower of Jesus. Because of Jesus, Paul had the desire and ability to do His will instead of working against God. And God's will for Paul was to become a great Christian missionary.

God wants us to put Him and His will for us first in our lives. He invites us to study His Word and to seek His will in prayer. Through His Spirit, God enables us to put Him first. Through His Son, God forgives us for those times when we sin and put other things before Him.

God is first to listen, forgive, guide, and empower us to do His will. And when we follow God's guidance, He richly blesses us in our work to reach our goals.

Talk about it: What goals have you set for yourself? How will you put God first in what you do with your life?

Prayer: Dear Father, thank You for always listening to me. Help me always to first seek You and Your will, and then follow it. I ask this in Jesus' name. Amen.

Moses Leads God's People | Exodus 1–4

Jacob's family of seventy people moved to Egypt at the invitation of Joseph and Pharaoh. As time and generations passed, the family grew in number. They became known as the people of Israel, with many thousands in population. A new Pharaoh made them slaves in Egypt. To weaken the strength of the Israelite nation, he ordered that all the Israelite baby boys be thrown into the Nile River and drowned.

But one Israelite mother took her baby and placed him into a basket. She set the basket in the river and prayed to God to protect him. Pharaoh's daughter discovered the baby in the basket and raised him as her son. She named him Moses.

When Moses had grown up, he saw an Egyptian mistreating an Israelite. Moses killed the Egyptian and ran into the wilderness to escape Pharaoh's anger. Years later, as Moses herded sheep on a mountainside, God spoke to him from a burning bush. The bush burned with fire, yet it didn't burn up.

God told Moses He had planned new things—an exciting future—for Moses. God did not want Moses to continue caring for sheep. Instead, God wanted Moses to care for His people. God wanted Moses to lead His people to freedom in the Promised Land.

Moses told God he wouldn't be able to do it. But God promised to be with Moses and to help him. God gave Moses the power to turn his rod into a snake as a sign of God's presence. When Moses argued that he was unable to speak well, God sent Moses' brother Aaron to help. Moses finally agreed. This was all part of God's plan to bring His people to the land in which Jesus, the Savior, would one day be born. Jesus would fulfill God's greatest plan—the plan for our eternal salvation.

New Things / Philippians 3:20

What will happen in the new year? The coming events are unknown. Some people like to guess what will happen in the future. These guesses are called predictions. Some predictions are wild guesses; others are based on information. Some predictions come true, but many do not.

In 1948, *Science Digest* predicted that "landing and moving around on the moon offers so many serious problems for human beings that it may take science another 200 years to lick them." In July 1969, just twenty-one years after this prediction, man walked on the moon for the first time.

The next time you get in the car, think of this prediction found in the 1889 *Literary Digest*: "The . . . horseless carriage [car] is a luxury for the wealthy . . . and will never come into as common use as the bicycle."

Of the thousands of predictions that have been made this century, some have come true, but many have been proven false.

The Bible has many predictions we call prophecies. Over three hundred prophecies were made about Jesus. Each one came true, just as God said it would. For example, the prophet Micah predicted not only Jesus' birth but also Jesus' birthplace: Bethlehem.

The Bible contains many predictions about Jesus' life, death, and resurrection, but it also has much to say about God's plans for our future. It says that all who believe in Jesus will not die but will live forever. It tells us that God has a plan for each of us and that nothing can ever separate us from the love of Jesus. It says that Jesus will go with us as we meet the joys and challenges of each new day of each new year! With Jesus, we can meet each new thing with confidence, knowing that God has all things under His control.

Talk about it: Look in your Bible for prophecies that have been fulfilled: Psalm 22:18 and John 19:23–24; Job 19:25–27 and John 11:23, 25–26; Psalm 47:5 and Mark 16:19. Write them down and compare them.

Prayer: Heavenly Father, thank You for the many promises and predictions You have given us. Help us always to trust in Your promise of salvation. Thank You for going with us into the new year and for all the blessings You give us with each new day. Amen.

Do all things without grumbling or disputing, that you may be blameless and innocent, children of God without blemish in the midst of a crooked and twisted generation, among whom you shine as lights. Philippians 2:14

The Wise Men Worship Jesus | Matthew 2:1–12

"Look at that star!" said the Wise Men. They studied stars, but they had not seen this one before. They knew this star was something special. "It must mean that a new king was born," they decided. God sent the star to lead the Wise Men to Jesus.

The Wise Men traveled many miles. Their trip took a long time. Finally, they got to the city of Jerusalem. The Wise Men asked, "Where is the one who has been born king of the Jews? We saw His star in the east and have come to worship Him."

Bad King Herod heard about the Wise Men. He told the Wise Men that he wanted to worship Jesus too. He lied. He really wanted to kill Jesus. The Wise Men went to the town of Bethlehem. They found Jesus there. The long trip was over!

They gave Jesus gifts that cost lots of money. They gave Him gold, frankincense, and myrrh. Then it was time to go. God warned the Wise Men not to tell Herod. God wanted to keep Jesus safe. Herod would not be able to destroy the plans God had for Jesus.

When Jesus grew up, He saved us and all people from our sins. Jesus was really a king—the king of the entire universe and everything in it.

Reversed! / Matthew 2:1–12

The letters were ready, and the children were ready. As each letter was held up, the children were to identify what the letter stood for: *S* is for *Savior*, *T* is for *tender*, *A* is for *amazing*, and *R* is for *royal*. The letters spelled *STAR*, a reminder of Jesus, who is called the "bright morning star."

Although the letters were supposed to spell *STAR*, there was a problem. The letters had accidentally been reversed when they were handed to the children, so instead of spelling *STAR*, they spelled *RATS*. People chuckled as the teacher quickly corrected the error.

But as the teacher thought about it, she discovered an important message. A star once led the Wise Men from a far-away land as they came to worship Jesus, the Savior of all people. When the devil saw the star and the men who followed the star to worship Jesus, he didn't rejoice; he said, "Rats!"

Jesus is the One whom God had promised would defeat the devil and pay the price for the sins of the whole world. Thank God that Jesus came to be our king. Thank God for the love of Jesus that shines from the cross and empty tomb. Thank God for the love of Jesus that still shines brightly today in the things His followers say and do to show others the way to Jesus!

Talk about it: How can you shine like a star, reflecting Christ's love at home? at school? in your neighborhood? What can you do to make a difference as you share His love?

Prayer: Dear Father, thank You for sending Your Son to defeat the devil so I can have forgiveness of my sins and eternal life. May the light of Jesus shine in my life and reflect His love to others. I ask this in His name. Amen.

In this is love, not that we have loved God but that He loved us and sent His Son to be the propitiation for our sins. Beloved, if God so loved us, we also ought to love one another. 1 John 4:10–11

Jesus Blesses the Little Children | Matthew 18:1–10; Luke 18:15–17

One day, the disciples asked Jesus, "Who is the greatest in the kingdom of heaven?" Jesus said, "You need to become like little children." Children believe in Jesus with their whole hearts. They know Jesus loves them. They don't worry about who is the greatest.

Another day, parents were bringing their children to Jesus so He could bless them. The disciples were upset and said, "Take these children away. We are busy with important things to do. Don't let your kids bother Jesus!"

Jesus didn't like what the disciples said. He said, "Let the little children come to Me, for the kingdom of heaven belongs to such as these." Jesus loved children. He wanted everyone to know that He came to save children too.

Jesus loves and cares for us, no matter how old we are, no matter what we look like, and no matter what we are able to do. Jesus loves us! He wants us to love and trust in Him in return. Because He loves us, we also love one another. Because of Jesus, we are all children of God.

The Love We Share / Luke 18:15–17

Five-year-old Donell had a grandfather who he thought was the best. On Saturdays, they always did something together. Sometimes, they played ball. Other times, they went to the park and played on the swings and the slide.

But the most fun for Donell were the special days when the two went fishing together. On those days, Grandpa baited Donell's hook and set Donell's bobber just right. He untangled Donell's line when it got knotted and did just about everything else that Donell needed done.

Grandpa told Donell where to throw his line, when to pull on the rod to hook the fish, and how to reel in the fish. It was a lot of work for Grandpa to go fishing with Donell, but he enjoyed it immensely.

"I love you, Grandpa," Donell said one day when the fish weren't biting., "I'm glad you like to go fishing with me, especially when you have to help me so much."

Grandpa replied, "I love you too, Donell. And because I love you, it makes me happy to help you." It made Grandpa feel good that he could help Donell when they went fishing.

The Bible teaches us about love. It tells us that God loved all people so much that He sent Jesus to become one of us. He showed His love by teaching people about God. He showed His love by obeying God in our place. And He showed His love by dying to take our sins away.

Our Bible reading for Valentine's Day reminds us that God loves all people, including those who are very young.

It doesn't matter how much or how little we can do on our own. Jesus loves us. And because Jesus loves us, we love one another. We show our love for others by helping them, as Jesus showed His love for us.

Jesus came to help us. He helped us with our problem of sin. Jesus did everything that needed to be done in order to take the punishment we deserve because of our sin. He hurt and died for us. That's love.

Talk about it: How do we know that God loves us? How can we share God's love with others?

Prayer: Dear Savior, may we always see You with the eyes of a child, trusting that Your words and promises are true. We love You because You first loved us. Amen.

Repentance and forgiveness of sins should be proclaimed in His name to all nations. Luke 24:47

Jonah and the People of Nineveh | Jonah 1–4

Ash Wednesday marks the beginning of the season of Lent. Lent is a time of repentance. During the weeks of Lent, God's people think about their life and the sins they have committed. These are the sins for which Jesus suffered and died.

Lent is also a time to focus on God and His deliverance. Long ago, the prophet Jonah experienced a unique kind of deliverance. Jonah had disobeyed God's command to go and preach repentance to the people of Nineveh. Instead, Jonah boarded a boat and headed in another direction.

But no one can run away from God. When a storm came up, the sailors with Jonah on the boat threw Jonah into the water in order to calm the storm. Then God delivered Jonah in an amazing

way. He sent a huge fish to swallow Jonah. Jonah remained inside the fish for three days.

Do you know what Jonah did while he was inside the fish? He thanked God for saving him. After three days, the fish placed Jonah on the shore, and Jonah went to preach to the people of Nineveh. The people listened to Jonah's words about their sins. And they repented.

To show their repentance, the people wore sackcloth and put ashes on their face. The ashes that people sometimes receive in worship on Ash Wednesday remind us that we too need to repent so that we may receive the forgiveness Jesus earned for us with His suffering and death. And the three days Jonah spent inside the fish? Jesus compared them to the three days He spent in the grave before returning to life on Easter Sunday!

It's Time to Give Up / Joel 2:13

Ash Wednesday is the first day of Lent. Today and all through Lent, we remember how Jesus suffered and died for us. Some people like to give up something they enjoy during the weeks of Lent. They feel that not eating chocolate or missing a TV show will remind them, in a small way, of how much Jesus suffered for them on the cross.

If you want, go ahead and give up something you like during Lent, because it is a good and beneficial Christian practice—vegetables, homework, and chores don't count. But God's prophet Joel suggests you give up other things as well.

In biblical times, God's people sometimes gave up a clean appearance and put ashes on themselves. They also wore rough cloth made from goat or camel hair. They felt that wearing the scratchy cloth, called "sackcloth," would show God how sorry they were for their sins. Sometimes, they even tore their clothing to show how sorry they were. But Joel says, "Rend your hearts and not your garments. Return to the Lord your God, for He is gracious and merciful, slow to anger, and abounding in steadfast love" (Joel 2:13).

God doesn't command that we wear ashes on Ash Wednesday. Neither does He require that we wear certain types of clothes to show how repentant we are. God looks at our heart. He turns our heart away from sin. He tells us to leave our sins at the cross, where Jesus died to take the punishment for them. As we leave our sins at the cross, we can go forward in joy and peace, knowing our sins are behind us.

~~~~~~~~~~~~~~~~~~~~

Talk about it: Write down on a scrap of paper a sin that's been bothering you. Throw the scrap in the trash. This activity can remind you of Christ's forgiveness. Thank God for taking all your sins away because of Jesus.

Prayer: Dear God, during this Lenten season, help me to turn my heart to You. Forgive my sin and fill me with Your joy and peace. In Jesus' name I pray. Amen.

Come to Me, all who labor and are heavy laden, and I will give you rest.
Matthew 11:28

In the Garden of Gethsemane | Matthew 26:14–16, 47–56

After Jesus chose His disciples, He taught them about the coming of God's kingdom. He told them plainly that He would suffer and die for the sins of the world. He traveled the land teaching and healing the sick.

Finally, the time came for Jesus to fulfill all things. He entered Jerusalem, taught in the temple, and gave His disciples the Lord's Supper. Then they went to a garden known as Gethsemane. Earlier, Judas, one of Jesus' disciples, had gone to Jesus' enemies and asked what they would give him if he would arrange for them to capture Jesus. Jesus' enemies agreed to give Judas thirty pieces of silver.

In the garden, when Jesus had finished praying and was talking with the disciples who were with Him, Judas came with soldiers to arrest Jesus. Judas identified Jesus from among the disciples by way of a prearranged signal. Judas called Jesus "Rabbi" and then leaned forward and kissed Him. When the soldiers arrested Jesus, His disciples all ran away.

With the arrest began Jesus' hours of suffering and death to pay for the sins of the world. We remember these hours of Jesus' suffering with a special season of the Church Year known as Lent.

Time-Out! / Matthew 11:25–30

The whistle blew! The referee hollered, "Time out, Blue." The basketball game came to a standstill, and everyone got to rest. The teams could get drinks and rethink their strategies. The fans could relax for a while before resuming their loud encouragement for the players.

"It's recess time!" has been the happy cry in schools all over the world. Students and teachers need some free time to release energy and frustration.

Jesus also became weary at times and went off by Himself to rest. In Scripture, we read that He sometimes left His disciples and the crowds so He could retreat to a quiet spot to rest. But He did more than rest—He prayed.

Jesus had been given the hardest job in history. He was to live a perfect life, and Satan was trying hard to ruin it. Jesus was to die an innocent, painful death, loaded down with the sins of the whole world.

Jesus was true man. That means He grew weary from doing His preaching and miracles. When people didn't listen to Him, He became sad. It would have been very easy, very human, to strike out in some way. But Jesus didn't. Instead, He came to His heavenly Father and the Spirit for help. By His faithfulness to the tasks before Him, He won salvation for us.

Lent is a season in the Church Year. The Church Year is built on events that are important in the lives of Christians. During Advent, we remember how people longed for the promised Savior, and we prepare for His coming at Christmas. During Lent, we remember why Jesus died on the cross.

The season of Lent offers a type of time-out for the people of God. It's a time to reflect on our sins and on the Savior's suffering and death to take those sins away. But we can take a time-out any time of the year. Whenever things get overwhelming, we can find rest in the Lord. We can pray. We can remember our Savior and His great love for us—a love that took Him to the cross, where He died for our sins, and to an empty tomb, where He showed He had won the victory over all that is evil and bad. As we read God's Word and meditate on it, we find rest and refreshment.

~~~~~~~~~~~~~~~

Talk about it: For what do you sometimes need a time-out?

Prayer: Dear Jesus, our refuge, lead us to restful things and places. Lead us always closer to You. Only there can we truly receive the refreshment we need. In Your name we pray. Amen.

"Blessed is the King who comes in the name of the Lord!
Peace in heaven and glory in the highest!" Luke 19:38

Jesus Rides into Jerusalem | Luke 19:28–40

On the Sunday before Jesus was to die for the sins of the world, He rode into the city of Jerusalem on a donkey. People lined the road to welcome Him.

They greeted Him as a king would be greeted. Many in the crowd spread their cloaks on the road. Still others got branches from the trees and spread them on the road. The people cheered Jesus on with the words "Hosanna to the Son of David! Blessed is He who comes in the name of the Lord! Hosanna in the highest!"

Jesus is a king even today. Long after He suffered, died, and rose again to pay for our sins, Jesus rules the entire universe, holding all things together by His almighty power.

What Kind of King? / Matthew 27:11; Revelation 17:14

Caleb was excited. He held the palm branch tightly in his hand. Shading his eyes from the sun, he looked down the narrow, dusty road. The king was coming! His parents spoke often of the new king, Jesus. Now he would see Him for himself.

Soon a donkey came into view. A man in a white robe rode on its back. Caleb dropped his palm in disappointment. This man didn't look like a king. He wore no royal robe; He had no crown. Whoever heard of a king riding on a scrawny, little donkey? His mother and father must be wrong. Certainly this Jesus was not the king.

Caleb and many others in Jerusalem that first Palm Sunday wanted an earthly king. They wanted a king who would free them from their Roman rulers. They wanted a king who would clothe and feed them. They wanted someone to make all their wishes come true.

But Jesus wasn't a king like other kings. Soon after Palm Sunday, Jesus told Pilate, "My kingdom is not of this world" (John 18:36). He came to earth not to give us everything we want, but to give us something better. He came to set us free from sin. He lived and died so we could be in His heavenly kingdom. He did more than any earthly king could do.

Sometimes, we may also want Jesus to be a magical servant who grants our every wish. We want Him to give us A's on tests and sunshine on the day of our ball game. We are disappointed if He doesn't do things our way. Although Jesus cares about our needs and wants, He is more concerned about our souls. He calls us to repentance and faith.

Jesus wants us to get excited about the spiritual things He cares so much about. He points us to our real home, heaven, where He reigns forever as King of kings.

~~~~~~~~~

Talk about it: Write down all the words you can think of that describe what a king is like. How does Jesus' kingship fit those words? How is it different?

Prayer: Lord Jesus, I am glad You are the heavenly King who gave Your life for me. Amen.

Peter Denies Jesus Three Times | Matthew 26:69–75

Jesus was busy the night on which He was betrayed. Earlier in the evening, He gave the disciples His body and blood with the bread and wine in the first Lord's Supper. Then, He had a time of great agony and struggle as He prayed in the garden of Gethsemane. He was betrayed by Judas into the hands of His enemies. His disciples deserted Him and fled.

But Peter was curious about what was happening to Jesus. From a distance, He followed Jesus and those who arrested Him. Peter sat outside the court where Jesus was on trial, hoping to find out what was happening to Jesus. Inside, a mockery of a trial was taking place. Jesus was being humiliated as soldiers were spitting on Him and hitting Him.

Outside, Peter was in the company of the soldiers and servants who served the officials. A servant girl spoke to Peter, saying she recognized him as a follower of Jesus. Then, another made the same accusation. Peter denied it both times. When other bystanders charged Peter as being a follower of Jesus, Peter swore he did not know Jesus.

When Peter heard a rooster crow, he remembered the words Jesus spoke earlier. Jesus had said that before the rooster would crow Peter would deny three times ever knowing Jesus. Realizing his sin, Peter went out and wept bitterly.

Rooster Reminder / Luke 22:31–34

Weather vanes have been around for almost two thousand years. The first known weather vane was on top of a temple in Greece. Later, weather vanes spread throughout Europe.

During the Middle Ages, weather vanes were mounted only on castles and cathedrals. Ninth-century church leaders required that every weather vane be in the shape of a rooster. Why a rooster? A rooster would remind people not to deny their faith, as Peter did.

Remember the story? It was on the Thursday evening before Jesus died on the cross. He and His disciples shared the Passover meal and the first Lord's Supper.

Then Jesus told Peter He was praying for him. Peter didn't think he needed that prayer. He thought he was strong. He told Jesus he was ready to die with Him. Peter said he was strong, but he was wrong. He was afraid to stand up for Jesus. He was afraid to speak up for Jesus.

The rooster on the weather vane is a reminder: don't be like Peter! Don't think you're brave enough to stand up for Jesus all by yourself. There might be a time when it is hard to say you are a Christian.

Jesus knows we need His help to keep our faith strong. He also knows we need His forgiveness when we fall into sin. He gives us courage to confess that He died for us. He gives us forgiveness so we can know that He still loves us, even when we are weak and deny Him. In prayer, ask Him to help you be faithful. Then rely on His strength to keep you faithful.

Talk about it: When Peter was in the high priest's courtyard, why was it hard for him to say he loved Jesus? When might it be hard for you to say Jesus is your Savior? Did Jesus forgive Peter for denying Him? Would He forgive you?

Prayer: Give me courage, Lord, to say I am Yours. As you forgave Peter, forgive me when I trust in my own strength or when I deny You. Amen.

155

Christ redeemed us from the curse of the law by becoming a curse for us—for it is written, "Cursed is everyone who is hanged on a tree." Galatians 3:13

Jesus Dies on a Cross for Us | Matthew 26:47–27:66

When Jesus was arrested in the garden of Gethsemane, the soldiers took Him to the palace of the high priest, Caiaphas. The high priest asked Jesus if He was the Christ, the Son of God. Jesus said, "You have said so." Caiaphas tore his robes in anger. Those assembled spit on Jesus and hit and mocked Him.

Early the next morning, the chief priests and elders of the people bound Jesus and led Him away to the Roman governor, Pontius Pilate, because they did not have the authority to sentence Him to death. Pilate questioned Jesus, asking Him whether He was the king of the Jews. Jesus answered by explaining that His kingdom is not of this world.

Pilate saw no reason that Jesus deserved to die. He came up with a plan. Pilate allowed the people to choose whether they wanted to free Jesus or a notorious criminal named Barabbas. But the people chose Barabbas.

When Pilate asked the people what He should do with Jesus, they shouted back, "Crucify Him!" Pilate took water and washed his hands before the people, explaining that he did not want the dirt of the sentencing of this innocent man on himself. Then He had Jesus whipped. The soldiers hurt and mocked Jesus by putting a crown of thorns on His head and placing a purple robe on Him. They spit on Him and continued to beat Him. Finally, they led Jesus away to be crucified.

They nailed Him to a cross made from two pieces of wood. Here, Jesus died for your sins and mine. Witnessing Jesus' crucifixion, a Roman centurion exclaimed, "Surely this is the Son of God!" After Jesus had died, a soldier pierced Jesus' side with a spear to make sure He was dead. Then Jesus' friends got permission to take His body down from the cross. They buried Jesus in a tomb and sealed the doorway with a large stone. But the tomb could not hold Jesus for very long! Soon, Jesus would arise, defeating death, just as He defeated sin and the devil for you and for me.

The Wondrous Cross / Galatians 6:14

When Jesus lived on earth, a cross was a horrible thing. No one would ever have worn a cross as jewelry or displayed it. The cross was a place of terrible punishment for the very worst criminals. It was horrendous to be nailed to a cross and to hang there until death. But Jesus willingly did this for us! Jesus never sinned, so He didn't die because of something He had done wrong. Jesus did it out of love. He died this horrible death to free us from all of our sins.

There is a hymn written more than two-hundred years ago that talks about the cross. The hymn is called "When I Survey the Wondrous Cross," and it was written by Isaac Watts. In this hymn, Watts pictured himself at the foot of the cross. He wrote as if he were with Mary and John looking at the crucified Jesus.

At first, people who heard this hymn were angry. They thought it was wrong of Isaac Watts to write in this way. The hymn was criticized as too personal. But Jesus' death *is* personal. He died for each of us—you and me! The hymn survived and is still sung in many churches, especially on Good Friday.

Today, the cross has become something beautiful for Christians. Crosses are found in our churches and homes. We may wear a cross around our neck. The cross changed from a horrible thing to a good thing because of Jesus. Now we think of Jesus' love and forgiveness when we see a cross.

Talk about it: What do you think of when you see a cross? How can you use a cross to tell others about Jesus?

 *Prayer: Lord Jesus, what a great and awesome Savior You are! You suffered and died the death I should have died because of my sins. Forgive me, Lord, for all I have done wrong. Help me to live for You. I ask this in Your holy, precious name. Amen.*

Jesus' Tomb Is Empty! | Matthew 28:1–10; John 20:1–9

After Jesus died on the cross, His friends buried Him in a new tomb and rolled a stone in front of the entrance. After the Sabbath, some of the women who followed Jesus went to His tomb to anoint His body. They went to the tomb about sunrise.

Meanwhile, there was an earthquake as an angel of the Lord came down from heaven. The angel rolled back the stone from the tomb and sat upon it. His appearance was like lightning. The soldiers guarding the tomb shook and fell over as if they were dead. When Mary Magdalene saw that the stone had been rolled away, she ran to Peter and John and told them, "They have taken the Lord out of the tomb, and we don't know where they have laid Him."

Entering the tomb, the other women saw an angel, who said, "Do not be afraid; for I know you are looking for Jesus. He is not here, for He is risen. Go quickly and tell His disciples that He has risen from the dead." The women ran back to the city. They were afraid, yet filled with joy. They ran to tell the disciples what they had seen and heard.

Jesus rose from the dead. Someday, we too will have a resurrection day! Jesus will bring us back from death to life, just as He brought His own body back from death to life.

Empty! / 1 Corinthians 15:20–23

Most things in this life are better when they are full. We like a full glass of lemonade and a full piggy bank. We are disappointed if we don't have a full stomach at the end of a meal.

There are some things, though, that are better when they are empty. A pencil sharpener can't do its job well unless it is emptied of its shavings. An empty backpack at the end of the day means no homework. An empty trash can means you won't have to take out the garbage for a while.

But do you know what the very best empty thing is? It is Jesus' tomb! The tomb was full on Good Friday. It held Jesus' lifeless body. The disciples didn't expect the grave to be empty on Easter Sunday. The women didn't, either. They came with spices to put on Jesus' body. And then, what a surprise! What was supposed to be full of death was empty!

But there is more good news about the empty tomb.

Because Jesus' grave was empty, it means death isn't the winner anymore. Yes, we will die someday. But there is a surprise ahead for us too. Someday, Jesus will return. He will call us out of the grave. He will lift us up to heaven. Our tombs will be as empty as Jesus' grave was on Easter morning.

For Christians, *empty* is a wonderful word. An empty tomb means eternal life. Jesus rose from the dead, and we will as well. Hallelujah! Jesus is risen!

Talk about it: What would have happened if Jesus' tomb had not been empty on Easter Sunday? Why is eternal life so wonderful?

Prayer: I praise You, Lord, for having power over death. Thank You for leaving an empty tomb so I, too, can have eternal life. Amen.

[Christter] is at the right hand of God, . . . interceding for us. Romans 8:34

Jesus Ascends into Heaven | Acts 1:1–11

Jesus visited with His disciples many times after Easter. He wanted to get them ready for a big job. They were to tell everyone about His free gift of salvation.

For forty days, Jesus met and spoke with His disciples about the coming kingdom of God. Jesus gave them work to do. He told them to go into all the world and to baptize and teach the people. He promised that He would be with them always.

Now, it was time for Him to leave. Jesus had finished His work on earth. He had died to take away our sins. He had come alive again to show His power over death. He had spent time with His disciples to make their faith stronger. It was time for Him to return to heaven.

Jesus took His disciples to a high hill. He said, "I will send the Holy Spirit to you. The Holy Spirit

will help you tell others about Me." As Jesus spoke these words, He began to rise from the ground. Jesus rose higher and higher into the sky until He rose above a cloud and the disciples could see Him no longer. Then two angels appeared among them and told them that Jesus would one day come back to earth in the same way as they had seen Him leave it.

Today, we are still waiting for Jesus to return. He reigns in heaven, where He is seated at the right hand of God the Father. There, He speaks to His Father for us. He tells His Father that we are holy in spite of the wrong things we do. We are holy because Jesus has made us holy. He has earned our holiness through His life, death, and resurrection.

Always with Us / Acts 1:6–11

Eric stared out the window at the sunny blue sky, remembering all the fun times he'd had during the summer. Today would be a perfect day for baseball! And here he was sitting in school, half listening to his teacher talk about all the great subjects they'd studied this year.

I'd rather be playing baseball, Eric thought. Schoolwork is too hard.

The teacher's voice interrupted his daydreaming. "Please, students, always remember to raise your hand when you want to answer a question." She wrote the word *always* on the board for emphasis.

Always—*where else have I seen that word recently?* Eric wondered. A moment later, he remembered. His Sunday School teacher had written their memory verse on the board last Sunday: "And behold, I am with you always" (Matthew 28:20).

She had explained that before Jesus rose into heaven, He promised to remain with us at all times. He lived and died for us all so that we can live with Him always in heaven.

Eric's thoughts were racing: *Jesus is with me always! That means He was with me when I struck out in June and when I hit that home run in July. And He'll be with me now as I do my schoolwork.*

Talk about it: Name some times and places when you're especially happy that Jesus is with you. How does His being with you help you?

Prayer: Dear Jesus, thank You for speaking to Your heavenly Father about the forgiveness and holiness we have in You. Keep us in Your loving care. Thank You for being with us always. Amen.

And it shall come to pass afterward, that I will pour out My Spirit on all flesh. Joel 2:28

The Disciples Speak in Many Languages

Acts 2

Before Jesus ascended into heaven, He told His disciples to remain in Jerusalem until the time when the Father would send them His Holy Spirit. Ten days after Jesus ascended, the disciples were in Jerusalem, waiting. It was Pentecost, a day of celebration. Jewish people from all over the world had come to Jerusalem to worship God. Jesus' followers were together in one place.

Suddenly, a mighty rushing wind came from heaven, and divided flames seemed to rest on each of Jesus' followers. Then they began to speak in languages they had not learned. These things happened as the Holy Spirit came upon God's people as Jesus had promised.

Peter stood up and began to preach a powerful sermon. He told the people about their sin. Then he told them about Jesus and His suffering, death, and resurrection. When the people heard these words, they were very moved. "What shall we do?" they asked. "Repent and be baptized in the name of Jesus for the forgiveness of sins," Peter answered. And that day about three thousand people were baptized. And so the Christian Church came into being at Pentecost.

Tell the Good News / Acts 2:1–41

Imagine this: you're going to appear on television! A talent agent saw you walking out of school and decided that you had excellent feet. So she asked you to make a shoe commercial to be seen on national television. This was such good news that you had to tell everyone. You called all your friends and relatives to tell them the good news.

Good news must be told. That's how it was on Pentecost, almost two thousand years ago. Only a small number of people knew what Jesus had done for them. Most of them spoke the same language, so people in other lands had little chance of hearing the Good News.

God took care of that problem. He sent the Holy Spirit to His followers and enabled them to speak in languages they hadn't known before. Those who received this power proclaimed news of the Savior to everyone who would listen.

Wouldn't it be awesome if you had that power? You can't expect another Pentecost, so if you want to tell others about Jesus in their own language, you'll have to learn it the normal way. You can tell others about Jesus right now, though—speaking the language God gives you.

And the Holy Spirit will help you. He will give you the words to use to tell others that God loves them and that Jesus died to take away their sins. You can pray that missionaries will continue to work with people who don't know Jesus. You also can ask the Holy Spirit to soften the hearts of those who oppose God and open the hearts of those who hear God's Word.

Talk about it: List ways you could help spread God's Word in your neighborhood.

Prayer: Send Your Holy Spirit, Lord, so I can help others know about their Savior. I pray this in Your holy name. Amen.

In all these things we are more than conquerors through Him who loved us.
Romans 8:37

David Fights the Giant Goliath | 1 Samuel 17

In Old Testament times, when King David was a boy, his father sent him with food for the army of God's people. David was also to see how things were going with the war. When David arrived at the battlefield, he saw an amazing sight. A Philistine giant named Goliath was challenging God's people to send out a champion to fight him.

No one would agree to fight such a powerful giant. But David said, "Who is this Philistine that he should defy the armies of the living God?" David said he would go to fight the giant. David explained that he had often had to fight lions and bears when he was working as a shepherd caring for his father's sheep. David trusted in God. He said, "The LORD who delivered me from the paw of the lion and from the paw of the bear will deliver me from the hand of this Philistine."

David chose five smooth stones from the brook. Then he went onto the battlefield armed only with his staff and sling and the power of God. Goliath expected a champion fighter to come against him. No doubt he was surprised at David's youth and size. He made fun of David. But David said, "This day the LORD will deliver you into my hand. . . . For the battle is the LORD's, and He will give you into our hand." David then took a stone and slung it at Goliath. The stone hit Goliath in the forehead, and he fell down dead.

Young people who stand before God's altar and pledge to remain faithful to their God and Savior can remind us of David. The power we take with us into life to face our challenging "giants" is the same power of God that went with David onto the battlefield to strengthen and encourage David and bring him victory. It is the power of God that has already won our greatest victory for us when Jesus defeated sin, death, and the devil on the cross.

Are You Growing? / 2 Thessalonians 1:1–4

How tall are you? Is there a place in your home where you measure and mark your height each year? Are you taller or shorter than other people your age? How about your spiritual growth? How is it doing? Do you measure it regularly? Jesus wants all of us, children and adults, to keep growing in our relationship with Him throughout our lives.

Growth in Jesus comes through God's Word and Sacraments. Weekly and daily worship reminds us of Jesus' great sacrifice for us on the cross. Recalling our Baptism reminds us that we have all the benefits of Christ's sacrifice—forgiveness of sins, rescue from death and the devil, and eternal salvation.

As we focus on God's love for us, we grow. The changes inside us may not be noticed over days or weeks. But through the months and years, God's Spirit will strengthen our relationship with Jesus. He will make us stronger when temptation and trouble come. We will know more of what God would have us do. We will more easily share His love with others. "Thanks be to God, who gives us the victory through our Lord Jesus Christ" (1 Corinthians 15:57).

Confirmation is a unique time in the life of a young person. It begins with a time of study of God's Word. Usually, this study is led by the pastor. During this time, a young person has the chance to ask questions about both the Bible and what it means to live for Jesus. At the end of this time of study, the young person usually stands before the congregation and promises to remain faithful to Jesus as his or her Savior. Then he or she is welcomed into congregational membership.

Confirmation can be a time of great growth in both understanding and faith. God helps us grow in many ways!

Talk about it: How does talking with your parents and others about your faith in Jesus help you? How are daily devotions and church services like appointments with God? How are they helpful to you?

Prayer: Dear Jesus, my Savior, I want to grow closer to You and be more like You. Send Your Spirit to live in me and to help me be strong in faith. Amen.

Go therefore and make disciples of all nations, baptizing them in the name of the Father and of the Son and of the Holy Spirit.

Matthew 28:19

Stephen's Vision of Heaven | Acts 6–7

Although the word *Trinity* does not appear in the Bible, it is a very important word to us, because Scripture teaches us that God has three persons—Father, Son, and Holy Spirit. Still, there remains only one God. This three-in-one aspect of God is a divine mystery. One of the places where the Bible clearly shows the presence of all three persons in the Trinity is at the death of Stephen.

Stephen was a faithful servant of God. He did miracles and great things among the people. But Stephen also had enemies. These were people who did not believe in Jesus, and they hated those who followed Him. These enemies told lies about Stephen. They said they had heard Stephen speak against Moses and against God. They stirred up the people and their leaders. Finally, Stephen was brought to trial before the ruling council. Those

on the council looked at Stephen and saw that his face was radiant like the face of an angel. They asked Stephen about the charges against him.

Stephen answered with a sermon. Stephen pointed out the people's sin. He told them about Jesus. He told the people that they had killed the Messiah God had sent to save them. Stephen's words made his enemies very angry. But Stephen was full of the Holy Spirit; he looked up into heaven and saw Jesus standing at the right hand of God the Father.

When Stephen told the enemies about what he was seeing, they took him out of the city and threw stones at him to take his life. When he was about to die, Stephen fell to his knees and prayed in a loud voice, "Lord, do not hold this sin against them." Then Stephen died.

The Holy 3-in-1 / Mark 1:9–11

Do you know any words in sign language? Here's a special word sign that means "Trinity."

Hold your left hand in front of you as if you're holding a glass. (Your thumb and fingers make a shape like a C.) With your right hand, hold up your thumb and the next two fingers, with the inside of your hand facing you.

Bring your right hand that says 3 down through your C-shaped hand. Then change your right hand from 3 to 1, pointing just your first finger. Bring the 1 up in front of your left hand.

That's it: 3-in-1. The Trinity! We believe in the Trinity: God the Father, Son, and Holy Spirit. They are three persons, but only one God.

God the Father made the world and takes care of us. Jesus, the Son of God, came to earth, died for our sins, and came back to life. The Holy Spirit gives us faith and dwells in our hearts.

Today, people speak, hear, and read the Good News about Jesus in many different languages. The language of signs is one of these languages. But no matter what language we use, we can't really understand the Trinity. God is beyond what we can say with human languages. We simply believe in the Trinity and worship our God, who is 3-in-1.

Glory be to God the Father,
Glory be to God the Son,
Glory be to God the Spirit:
Great Jehovah, Three in One!

Talk about it: Look around in your church for symbols of the Trinity. You might see a triangle or a design with three circles.

Prayer: We praise You, Holy Trinity, for creating us and for giving us our family, friends, and all we have, for saving us from our sins and for forgiving us and opening heaven to us, and for giving us the power and desire to live for You. Thank You, God! We praise You in Jesus' name. Amen.

We were buried therefore with [Christ] by baptism into death, in order that, just as Christ was raised from the dead by the glory of the Father, we too might walk in newness of life. Romans 6:4

God's People Enter Canaan | Joshua 3–4

Long ago, God's people Israel wandered in the wilderness for forty years. After this, the Lord led His people across the Jordan River and into Canaan, the land He had promised to give them. Here, they would enjoy a new life. They would live in houses they had not built and harvest crops they had not planted.

Their entrance into the Promised Land happened like this: When the feet of the priest who carried the mercy seat of God, the ark of the covenant, touched the Jordan River, the waters parted and the ground under the river became miraculously dry. The priests carrying the ark stood in the middle of the dry riverbed while all the people crossed over. Then they carried the

ark onto the riverbank, where the people had gone. When the feet of the priests carrying the back of the ark touched the riverbank and all had safely crossed, the waters of the river returned and began to flow as normal once again.

When we begin anything new, we can remember how God makes us new in Baptism, when we too pass through waters connected to God's Word. Through Baptism, God makes us new people, people forgiven in Jesus and welcomed into a new life as members of God's family. Here, we, too, daily experience newness of life, knowing Jesus has forgiven our sins. We have a new life to live for Jesus and an eternal home in heaven awaiting us.

A Fresh Start / Psalm 103:9–12

Happy New Year! Don't worry; you haven't been asleep for months—it's not January. But it is a new year in school.

If you are like most students, the beginning of the new school year is exciting. You have new clothes, new pencils, and new books. It's a time for a fresh start, and you have high hopes for the new year.

But after a few weeks of school, things may seem a little less exciting. You may even feel a little disappointed. Your new shoes will become scuffed, your pencils worn to short stubs. Some lessons may be troublesome. Perhaps you even worry about getting bad grades. Or you worry about getting into trouble trying too hard to get others to like you. Does some of this sound like your school experiences?

In some ways, everyday life is like the beginning of a school year. We get excited about doing something, and we want it to go well. Then we goof up, and things don't turn out the way we had planned. We feel like we need to start over.

We Christians want to please God and obey Him. We might try hard to do what is right, but then we sin and things get messed up. Because of Jesus, our sins are forgiven and God gives us a fresh start. You may get only one fresh start for each school year. But God gives you many fresh starts each day. Now, that's really exciting!

Talk about it: What are some things at school that may tempt you to sin? When you think about the bad things you have done, how does knowing God forgives all your sins make you feel? How can you serve and obey God in school?

Prayer: Dear Jesus, You went to school when You were growing up too. Help me follow Your example and be a good student. Thank You for giving me a fresh start by forgiving my sins. Amen.

God opposes the proud but gives grace to the humble. 1 Peter 5:5

The Pharisee and the Tax Collector in the Temple | Luke 18:9–14

We may think that God has saved us **because of how good we are.** But God tells us in His Word that we are all sinners. And we are saved because of Jesus. Jesus obeyed God in our place. Then He took our punishment and died on the cross to take our sins away.

Jesus once told a story to teach us about the danger of thinking we are good. Jesus told of two men who went into the temple to pray. One of the men was a Pharisee and the other was a tax collector. The Pharisee stood apart from others as if to draw attention to himself. He prayed, "God, I thank You that I am better than people who steal, cheat, and do other bad things, or even better than people like this tax collector."

But the tax collector stood in a place where he might not be noticed. He bowed his head humbly and said, "God be merciful to me, a sinner!" Jesus commented that the tax collector's way was the right way. He prayed knowing he needed God and His mercy and love.

We cannot save ourselves. No one can. Instead, we need the gifts of forgiveness, new life, and a home in heaven that God offers us freely in Jesus.

No More Indulgences / Romans 5:1–2

At the time of Martin Luther, the Christian church in Europe had invented something called "indulgences." These were pieces of paper that promised forgiveness of sins to people who bought them. If people did something especially sinful, they might buy an indulgence to make themselves feel better.

For those who had already died, a priest named John Tetzel said: "As soon as the coin in the coffer rings, the soul from purgatory's fire springs." Many people believed wrongly in a place called purgatory. Average Christians were said to go there after death to be purged, or cleansed. Tetzel asked people to give money so that their loved ones would get out of purgatory and into heaven.

Martin Luther saw this selling of indulgences as wrong. On October 31, 1517, he nailed ninety-five statements on a church door in Wittenberg, Germany. He said that the Bible does not tell us to rely on indulgences or anything we think we can do to earn forgiveness or goodness in the sight of God. Instead, the Bible teaches us to rely on the forgiveness Jesus earned by living and dying for us. The Bible tells us we are justified (or made good) by God's grace through faith alone. People cannot buy or earn their way to heaven. Heaven is a gift from God through the death of Jesus Christ on the cross.

When Luther was asked to take all this back, he said: "Here I stand. I can do no other. God help me. Amen." He was saying he had to teach what the Bible taught, not what people or the church decided to teach.

Remember this great Reformation theme from Romans 5:1: "Therefore, since we have been justified by faith, we have peace with God through our Lord Jesus Christ." Praise God that Christians believe this today.

Talk about it: What does the Reformation begun by Martin Luther mean in your life?

Prayer: Lord God, I love You so much. I pray that You will reform me every day to be more like You. Forgive me for trusting in myself and in how good I think I am. Teach me to rely more and more on You and Your goodness. Make me strong in what I believe and comfort me with Your love. In Jesus' name I pray. Amen.

The word of God . . . is at work in you believers. 1 Thessalonians 2:13

The Widow's Offering | Mark 12:41–44

People came to the temple to pray and worship God. Jesus was there too. He was watching people put their money gifts into the offering container. The rich people who came to the temple that day gave lots of money.

One woman stopped to give an offering. Her husband had died, so she was a widow. The woman was very poor. She reached deep into a small pouch. Her fingers pulled out two tiny coins. The coins were worth less than a penny. She dropped them into the offering box.

Jesus began talking to His disciples. He said, "Did you see how much money that widow gave to God? She gave a great gift. She gave the most. The rich people had lots of money to give. They will never miss the money they gave. But she gave everything she had."

God blessed the widow. She was not afraid to give money for God's work. She trusted God to give her what she needed.

God gives us everything we have. He gives us Jesus to be our Savior and friend.

Who's a Saint? / Revelation 21:4

On November 1, the Church celebrates a festival known as All Saints' Day. It is when we think of Christians who were on earth but now live with God in heaven. Maybe you have a grandparent, or another family member or friend, who is now a saint.

Does a person have to die to become a saint? No. You became one when God named you as one of His children by faith. For most of us, that happened when we were baptized.

What role do saints play in the life of believers? Living saints support and encourage us in the life we live for Jesus. They care enough about us to tell us when we are wrong. They remind us of God's love and promises when we are feeling sad or going through tough times.

Those saints who now live in heaven give us examples of how God's power moved them to live and act during their time on earth. The widow Jesus saw one day giving an offering in the temple is one example. Jesus commented on her willingness to give God all she had. Jesus marveled at her trust in God. Similarly, God wants us, His living saints, to rely on Him for everything. He will forgive our sins, He will give us all we need to live each day. And He will take us finally to live with Him in heaven.

So, on All Saints' Day, we think of millions of saints who have already died in Christ. But we can also think of ourselves and other followers of Jesus, saints still alive who will join them someday.

Talk about it: How might knowing that you are already a saint make a difference in the way you act?

Prayer: Praise to You, God, for the faithful witness of all the saints who have ever lived. Keep me strong in my faith in Jesus that someday I will be a heavenly saint. I ask this in Jesus' name. Amen.

> Give thanks to the LORD, for He is good;
> for His steadfast love endures forever.
> Psalm 118:1

The Thankful Leper

Luke 17:11–19

Once there were ten sick men. They had a skin sickness called leprosy. It was terrible. Other people did not want to be near them. The people were afraid they would catch the sickness. People with leprosy had to stay far away from healthy people.

Jesus was not afraid of people with leprosy. He loved them, just as He loved healthy people. Jesus was walking along a road one day. The ten men with leprosy shouted, "Jesus, Master, have pity on us!" Jesus felt sorry for them. Jesus told the sick men to go and show themselves to the priest. The priest was the one who decided whether sick people were well enough to return to their homes. While the men were on their way to see the priest, Jesus took away their sickness. Their skin became healthy. How happy they were to know that they could be with their families and friends again!

One of the men stopped running. He did not continue on his way to the priest. He turned around and ran back to Jesus. He thanked Jesus for taking away his leprosy.

Reflections of a Thankful Heart / 2 Corinthians 9:11–15

Try this experiment. Take two paper cups. Leave one white, but color the other cup with a black marker. Fill both cups with equal amounts of water (at the same temperature), and set them in the sun. After 30 minutes, compare the temperature of the water in the cups.

The color of the paper cups has had an effect on the amount of heat absorbed by the water. The black cup has absorbed heat, which raised the temperature of the water. The white cup reflected the heat and kept its contents cool. But no matter what the color of the paper cup is, it cannot create heat on its own. Heat must come from a different source—in this case, the sun. The color of the cup determines only where the heat will go.

Today, we remind ourselves to be thankful for the many blessings we receive every day from God. But what is the source of our thankfulness? Just as the cups cannot create heat, we cannot create thankfulness in our heart. Thankfulness is a blessing from God. And it is a special blessing because a thankful heart is a content heart.

When the gift of thankfulness fills our heart, we have acted as the black cup to absorb God's gift. He reminds us of His love and care for us and turns our hearts to Him with love and gratitude.

But thankfulness is more than something to be absorbed. We can also reflect thankfulness. When God's love fills our hearts, we respond with generosity toward other people in our lives. We can supply the needs of His people through gifts, acts of kindness, and words of love. His Word assures that our reflecting of thankfulness will result in more thanksgiving to God.

Talk about it: Make a list of ten things you would like to thank God for. How can you reflect thankfulness toward other people?

Prayer: Thank You for Your many blessings, Lord. Make my heart ready to absorb Your thankfulness and reflect Your generosity. In Jesus' name I pray. Amen.

When the fullness of time had come, God sent forth His Son, born of woman, born under the law, to redeem those who were under the law, so that we might receive adoption as sons. Galatians 4:4–5

Gabriel Announces the Coming of the Savior

Luke 1:26–38

At just the right time in human history, God sent the angel Gabriel to bring some important news to a young woman named Mary. The news: the time was right for God to send His Son to earth to save all people from their sins. The Savior would be the Son of God, but He would be born to Mary.

Mary asked the angel how such a wonderful, remarkable thing could happen. But the angel simply reminded Mary, "Nothing will be impossible with God." And so Mary waited for the baby Jesus to be born. She waited just as we wait to celebrate His birth during a period of waiting, called Advent.

Advent is a time of preparation for the coming of baby Jesus at Christmas. For the people of God, preparing for Christmas includes preparing our heart. We prepare our heart by repenting of our sins. God's Word tells us that Jesus came long ago in Bethlehem, but one day He will come again. This time, He will take us to live with Him forever in heaven.

Advent Adventure / Matthew 28:20

During Advent, we think of Jesus' coming. This season reminds us of the fact that He has already come and also that He will come again.

When we think of His first coming, we think of Mary and Joseph, shepherds and Wise Men. These people played an important role in the birth and first days of Jesus' life here on earth. They were all in their own ways involved in the great ADVENT-ure of the coming of the Christ Child.

An adventure may mean taking a risk or being exposed to danger. The people surrounding Jesus at His birth did indeed take risks. Mary and Joseph risked ridicule because of Mary's pregnancy. The shepherds risked being considered foolish for listening to angels singing in the night sky. The Wise Men risked their own lives by disobeying Herod.

Yet, each of these people willingly took part in the ADVENT-ure of Jesus' birth. Because of their faith in God's plan, they exposed themselves to danger.

Now, as we await the second coming of Christ, we are all involved in the ADVENT-ure. Each day, we face risks because of our faith in Jesus. When we stand up to our classmates and tell them we will not make fun of someone, we are taking a risk. When we invite a friend to be our guest at Sunday School, we are taking a risk. When we help someone who is unable to help himself or herself, we are taking a risk.

All of these times could seem very scary and overwhelming, just as they must have seemed to the first ADVENT-urers. But we have a Wonderful Counselor and a Mighty God. He promises in Matthew 28:20, "Behold, I am with you always, to the end of the age." In other words, He will be with us until the end of this earthly ADVENT-ure.

Talk about it: What adventures have you had because you believe in Jesus? List the letters in ADVENT. Try to write a promise from God that starts with each of the letters in ADVENT.

Prayer: Heavenly Father, thank You for being with me as I face my earthly ADVENT-ures. Help me prepare for Your coming. In Jesus' name I pray. Amen.

For unto you is born this day in the city of David a Savior, who is Christ the Lord. Luke 2:11

The Angels Announce to the Shepherds

Luke 2:8–21

God's Son was born to Mary when she and Joseph were away from home in Bethlehem. Because they had difficulty finding a place to stay, they finally ended up spending the night in a barn where animals were kept. Here, the Savior of the world was born!

In the fields outside Bethlehem, shepherds were watching their flocks. On Christmas night, the angel of the Lord suddenly appeared in glory and frightened them. But the angel told them not to be afraid. He told the shepherds that the Savior, Christ the Lord, had been born in Bethlehem.

Suddenly, a great number of angels appeared and joined the first angel praising God and saying, "Glory to God in the highest, and on earth peace among those with whom He is pleased!" When the angels went away, the shepherds quickly went to Bethlehem and found the baby lying in a manger, just as the angel had said. Then, filled with joy, the shepherds thanked and praised God and joyfully shared with others the news of these amazing events.

The Candy Cane / Luke 2:8–21

Have you eaten any candy canes lately? They're a favorite treat at Christmastime. We can use candy canes to tell people about Jesus' birth, life, and death.

Candy canes start as a stick of hard white candy. The white stands for purity. Jesus was born without sin. All people are born in sin. The sin that came into the world through Adam and Eve affects us all. It is our human condition, and it separates us from God. Jesus, however, was fully God as well as fully human; He was without sin.

The hardness of the candy cane reminds us of the firmness of God's love and promises.

Already in the Garden of Eden, God promised to send a Savior to take away our sins.

The shape of a candy cane reminds us of the letter *J*; the precious name of Jesus begins with a *J*. Jesus is the Savior God had promised to send.

The cane is also shaped like a shepherd's crook. The Bible calls Jesus the Good Shepherd. He cares for us, guides us, and protects us from evil, just as a shepherd cares for his sheep.

Finally, the red stripes on the candy cane symbolize Jesus' suffering and death. The small stripes stand for the stripes on His back when He was whipped by the soldiers. The large red stripe represents His blood, which was shed for us.

When Jesus died on the cross, He earned forgiveness for the sins of the world. Now we are no longer separated from God. His Spirit lives in us. We have the promise of eternal life.

What a sweet story of love there is in this sweet treat!

Talk about it: What are some things you can think about the next time you eat a candy cane? Give a friend a candy cane and share the story.

Prayer: Thank You, Father, for sending Your dear Son to suffer and die for me. Help me to always remember Your great love. In Jesus' name I pray. Amen.

Blessed be the God and Father of our Lord Jesus Christ! According to His great mercy, He has caused us to be born again to a living hope through the resurrection of Jesus Christ from the dead.

1 Peter 1:3

A Baby for Zechariah and Elizabeth | Luke 1:5–25

Every birth is an important birth. Every child is a gift from God. Shortly before the birth of Jesus, another special baby was born. His birth, like the birth of the Savior Himself, was told about hundreds of years before it actually happened. About this child the angel said, "He will go before [the Savior] in the spirit and power of Elijah . . . to make ready for the Lord a people prepared."

The birth of this special baby happened like this: Zechariah the priest was serving God in the temple when Gabriel, an angel of the Lord, appeared and told him that God had heard his prayers and that he and his wife, Elizabeth, would have a son. They were to name him John. Given their advanced age, Zechariah doubted Gabriel's words. Gabriel then told Zechariah he would not be able to speak until the baby was born.

The words of Gabriel came to be true. Soon after the visit of the angel, Elizabeth became pregnant, and with the passing of time, she gave birth to a son. The happy couple named their baby John. At the naming of John, Zechariah again became able to speak.

When the child grew up, he became known as John the Baptist. He preached repentance and baptized people in preparation for the coming of the Messiah. God had a plan for John's life.

Somewhat similarly, God has a plan for everyone. At each birthday, we remember God's grace and goodness as we celebrate another year of life. Like John, we ready ourselves for the coming of the Messiah. Unlike John, we await Jesus' second coming, the time when He will take us to live with Him in a happy home in heaven.

Chosen by Our Father / Deuteronomy 7:6–9

Davy's family was standing in front of the window in the hospital nursery, looking at the newborn babies. The babies were wrapped snugly in pink or blue blankets, sleeping peacefully. One baby, wearing nothing but a diaper, was lying under a bright light in a closed-in plastic box, apart from the rest.

Mother pointed to this baby and said, "Davy, that's your new baby sister, Cathy."

Davy looked at the scrawny baby that had many tubes and wires connecting her to machines. Her skin looked a little yellow. Then he looked at the other babies in their cozy blankets, "No, Mom. I want this one," Davy said, pointing to a baby in a pink blanket.

Father smiled and patted Davy's head. "Davy, we're not here to pick one out," he said gently. "God has given us this baby. She has a serious heart condition. And even though she isn't perfect, we've loved her since before she was born because she is ours. We can't wait until she is well so that we can take her home."

We all have much in common with Cathy. We are not perfect either. We were born with a condition called sin. We sin every day by the things we say and do. But God loves us anyway. He loves us so much that He sent His only Son to die for our sins. Jesus, God's perfect Son, forgives our sins so that someday we may live with our Father in heaven.

God loves us not because we are perfect but because He is our Father. He chose us to be His children even before we were born. And He loves us exactly the way we are.

Talk about it: Did God choose us because we were lovable? Did He choose us because He knew we would do good things? Then why did God choose us?

Prayer: Dear Father, thank You the gift of life. Thank You for choosing me to be Your child. Help me always remember that You loved me enough to send Your perfect Son to cancel my sins. In Jesus' name I pray. Amen.

For I know the plans I have for you, declares the Lord, plans for welfare and not for evil, to give you a future and a hope. Jeremiah 29:11

God's Plan for Moses and His People | Exodus 1–4

For many years, the people of Israel were held captive as slaves in Egypt. The king of Egypt put in place a plan to keep the people of Israel under control by making a law that all boy babies that were born were to be thrown into the Nile River.

But one woman who gave birth to a son refused to obey the wicked king. She made a tiny boat of reeds and pitch. Then she placed her baby in the boat and set it afloat in the waters of the Nile River. The baby's sister Miriam was to watch the baby as he floated in the little boat.

When the Egyptian princess, the king's daughter, came down to wash in the river, she saw the boat with the baby inside. The princess felt sorry for the baby when he cried. She decided to raise the baby as her son. We might say she adopted the baby. She named him Moses.

This adoption was part of God's plan so Moses would know the language and customs of the Egyptians. His Egyptian education and life in a palace would one day assist him in God's plan to rescue the Israelites. God had special plans for Moses and the future of the nation of Israel.

When Moses was a man, God called to him out of a bush that burned in flames but did not burn up. God told Moses he was the person God had chosen to lead His people to the Promised Land. God told Moses He would give him all he needed to lead God's people. God helped Moses to live out God's plan for his life. In a similar way, God will help each of us to live our lives for Him.

Look Around; Don't Worry! / Matthew 6:25–34

Siu Wan was worried. She had lived a pretty hard life so far. She could hardly remember her mother. What she mostly remembered was living in the street, pretty much alone, and never having enough to eat or wear. Finally, someone had found her and taken her to an orphanage.

Today, something exciting was going to happen. She was going to be adopted by a family. Today, she would meet them for the first time. She already knew that there were two other daughters in the family. They were both adopted too. She wondered if her new mother and father would have enough food to feed her in addition to the other children. She wondered if there would be enough clothes for her to wear or room for her in their house. That's why Siu Wan was worried.

When she first met her new family, she saw that her sisters were wearing very nice clothes. They looked like they had plenty to eat. They showed her a picture of their house. It looked like there was plenty of room for her too. In time, Siu Wan learned not to worry. She could see that her new parents took good care of her sisters, and she knew that they would take care of her too.

When we sometimes worry about whether God will take care of us, Jesus tells us to look around at some of God's other creations—the birds and flowers. He wants us to see how God takes care of them. When we see that, we'll remember that the same God takes care of us too. In Baptism, He has adopted us into His family. We are far more important to God than birds or flowers. He shows His love for us in Jesus, who came to be our Savior. That is why we never need to worry.

Talk about it: What does it mean to you that God has adopted you into His family?

Prayer: Dear heavenly Father, thank You for adopting me into Your family through Christ Jesus. Help me not to worry about things. Keep reminding me of Your love for me, and help me trust in You. I ask these things in Jesus' name. Amen.

Jesus Changes Water into Wine | John 2:1–11

A family is a group of people united by a common set of parents or grandparents. People in the same family may look alike and enjoy doing the same things. When at their best, family members show love and care for one another. They sometimes travel great distances to share important events. Some of these may be happy. Others of these may be sad.

Jesus is the Son of God. But Jesus also had a human family. Because Jesus is a man, He liked going to events with others in His family. One time, Jesus attended a wedding with His mother. Jesus' disciples were also there. Weddings in Bible times usually included parties that lasted many days.

During the wedding party, Mary came to Jesus to tell Him about a problem. The party was running out of wine. Mary then asked the servants to do whatever Jesus would tell them to do. Jesus saw six large stone jars. He told the servants to fill up the jars with water. After they filled the jars, Jesus told the servants to take some of the contents and give it to the person in charge of the party. The water in the jars had become wine. Jesus had done His first miracle.

The head of the banquet commented on this very good wine. "Usually, people serve the best wine at the beginning of the party," he said, "but you have kept the best wine until now."

By this miracle, Jesus showed that although He is a real man, He is also truly God. And even though Jesus is God, He cares about everything that troubles and concerns people, even things such as running out of refreshments at a party!

Nana's Quilt / Colossians 3:1–4

Amy's Nana made a quilt using family photos. When family members come to visit Nana, they reminisce about special days gone by as they look at the quilt. They say that all the baby pictures look alike. They laugh at snapshots of shaving-cream battles and muddy go-cart drivers. They smile at a little boy who wrapped himself in Christmas garland. And they ask about all the special people they don't recognize, people who lived long ago.

One day, granddaughter Amy asked Nana if she missed all those special people who had gone to be with Jesus. Nana said that she did miss them, but Nana told Amy that each one of them was a Christian—a child of God. She had a twinkle in her eye when she said that she knew she would see them again.

Nana's answer showed that her heart and mind were set on things above—on godly things. God gave Nana that new heart in her Baptism. Her faith in Jesus grew as she was strengthened through God's Word. Jesus helped her at very sad times and in times of trouble. And God will also help you to set your mind on things above while you live out each day of homework and practices, of book reports and family chores, of ups and downs.

Family is one of God's greatest gifts to us. Many enjoy the help and care of fathers and mothers who love them even as they love Jesus. But if we believe in Jesus, we are also members of another family—the family of God. This is the best of all families to belong to. It means we have God as our Father and none other than Jesus our Savior as our brother!

Talk about it: What do you like most about your family? Draw a picture of a quilt to represent your life and those who are important to you. Put at least four pictures in it. Put a cross at the center.

Prayer: Dear Jesus, thank You for dying on the cross to save all people. Thank You for my family. Help me to love and serve them. Help me to love and serve You all the days of my life. Amen.

God said, "Let the earth bring forth living creatures according to their kinds—livestock and creeping things and beasts of the earth according to their kinds." Genesis 1:24

God Provides for Elijah | 1 Kings 17:1–6

In the days of wicked King Ahab, the people of Israel fell away from God and worshiped false gods. God's prophet Elijah told Ahab that God was going to bring a drought upon the land.

Even though the lack of rain brought hardship upon the land and its people, God desired to work good through it, for God wanted the drought to remind people of their dependence on Him. God wanted the people to repent of their sin and come back to Him.

God told Elijah to stay at the brook Cherith. Here, Elijah drank from the brook, but God provided food for Elijah in a miraculous way. Ravens carried bread and meat to Elijah both morning and night.

Just as God blessed Elijah through the ravens at Cherith, God has blessed people in many ways with birds and other animals. Often, these animals have served us as friends and companions. When they die, we miss them.

Still, in Jesus, we have the best of all possible friends. And in His Word, He tells us that He will never leave us. He will help us deal with the sadness and loss we face at the death of our pets.

A Story about Scars / John 20:26–29

One day, a young boy named Matthew decided to walk his large dog, Ozzie, down the road. He loved to play with his dog, yet he was afraid that Ozzie would run away. He got a leash so he could walk Ozzie properly.

As they were going down the road, Matthew noticed that Ozzie was pulling on the leash very hard. One time, it almost came out of Matthew's hand, so he decided to wrap the leash around his arm as much as he could. The leash was tight around his arm, so he knew Ozzie could not get away.

Suddenly, a rabbit ran right in front of Ozzie. Ozzie pulled so hard that Matthew fell to his knees on the gravel road, and the pain was terrible. He was hurt so badly that he tried to let go, but he had wrapped the leash around his arm so tightly that he couldn't.

Finally, Matthew was able to let go of the leash, and Ozzie ran off into the woods. Matthew cried because his dog was lost and because his knees were bleeding. When he got home, his mom treated and bandaged his knees.

When his knees had healed, Matthew thought about what had happened. Even though he had a new dog, he still missed Ozzie. And even though his knees felt better, he still had scars on them.

It's interesting that when we have a scar on our body or a hurt feeling inside, we usually have a story to explain how it came about. When He was nailed to the cross for us, Jesus, too, received scars from His wounds. He has an explanation for us as to why He got those scars: He loves us.

When Jesus showed Thomas the nail marks in His hands and feet, He encouraged His disciple: "Do not disbelieve, but believe" (John 20:27). To us, too, the Savior says, "Believe that I received these scars for your sake. Trust Me for your salvation."

~~~~~~~~~~~~~~~~~

Talk about it: Can you share a time when your feelings were hurt or you got some scars? How does God help you recover from such bruises?

 *Prayer: Dear God, sometimes life isn't easy. But I know that You are always with me and that You send special people into my life to love me. Thank You for the grace and help You give me. In Jesus' name I pray. Amen.*

And no inhabitant will say, "I am sick"; the people who dwell there will be forgiven their iniquity. Isaiah 33:24

Jesus Heals the Crippled Man | Luke 5:17–26

Jesus is the greatest of all healers. He is a healer of both soul and body. Jesus once showed that He could heal both souls and bodies. It happened while He was teaching in a house.

The house was crowded with lots of people, including some who were Jesus' enemies. Some men came carrying a bed. On the bed was their friend; he could not walk. The men could find no way to get their friend into the house to see Jesus, so they went onto the roof of the house and lowered the man down before Jesus through a large hole they had made in the roof.

Jesus said to the sick man, "Your sins are forgiven you." When Jesus' enemies heard these words, they thought that Jesus might be pretend-ing He was God, since only God can forgive sins. Being God, Jesus knew their thoughts. He said, "Which is easier, to say, 'Your sins are forgiven you,' or to say, 'Rise and walk'? But that you may know that the Son of Man has authority on earth to forgive sins . . ." Jesus turned to the sick man and said, "I say to you, rise, pick up your bed and go home."

The sick man now could walk! He did as Jesus commanded. As he went his way, the man glorified God. Just as surely as Jesus forgave and healed the sick man in this story, Jesus remains the great healer today. He still forgives all sins and heals all diseases. What a great God and Savior Jesus is!

The Best Doctor / Isaiah 53:4—6

Dr. Byrum's office. How may I help you?" said the voice on the other end of the phone.

"I'd like to make an appointment to see the doctor. Do you have any openings on Friday morning?" Jack replied.

"Can you come at 10 o'clock?" the receptionist asked.

"That would be perfect," Jack answered.

The receptionist took Jack's name and phone number, and the conversation was over.

That Friday, Jack went to the doctor's office. It wasn't a big problem. The doctor took care of him, and soon he was on his way. As he was returning home, Jack realized how comforting it is to have a good doctor.

We Christians have an even better doctor. That doctor is God. God cured the world of the most awful disease—the disease of sin. He didn't cure sin by giving medicine. No one had to get a shot to be cured of sin. In fact, we didn't even have to contact the doctor to make an appointment.

God took care of everything. He looked at the sinful world and figured out how to do it all. Healing of body is a wonderful gift. But even more wonderful is the healing of the soul Jesus provided us through His life, death, and resurrection. Because of this healing, when God looks at us, He no longer sees people who have the sin they were born with or the sins they have done. He sees persons who have been washed clean by Jesus' blood. He sees children of God who are healed!

Talk about it: Tell about a time God healed you from a disease. Then talk about the time God healed you from sin-sickness. Talk about heaven, where there will be no kind of sickness—ever!

Prayer: Dear God, You are the best doctor in the world. You heal us both in body and in soul. You took care of our disease of sin by sending Your Son, Jesus. He took the punishment for us, and now we are healed. Thank You for making us perfect in Your sight. Amen.

I know that my Redeemer lives, and at the last He will stand upon the earth. And after my skin has been thus destroyed, yet in my flesh I shall see God, whom I shall see for myself, and my eyes shall behold, and not another. Job 19:25–27

Jesus Raises Jairus's Daughter

Luke 8:40–42, 49–56

Jesus is not afraid of death, for He has conquered and overcome it. Because we know and believe in Jesus, we need have no fear of death either.

Jesus once was returning from a trip when Jairus, a ruler at the synagogue, came up to Him. Falling at Jesus' feet, Jairus pleaded with Jesus to come to his house. His twelve-year-old daughter was very sick and was dying. Jesus agreed to go with Jairus.

While they were walking along, Jesus healed a woman who had been sick for many years. Just as Jesus finished healing the woman, someone from Jairus's house came with the sad news that the little girl had died. But Jesus told Jairus, "Do not fear; only believe, and she will be well."

When they arrived at the house, everyone was crying. Jesus said to them, "Do not weep, for she is not dead but sleeping." But the girl was really dead, and the people laughed at Jesus. Jesus took the girl by the hand and said, "Child, arise." With that, the girl came back to life and sat up.

For those who love and trust in Jesus, death is no more to be feared than sleep. One day, Jesus will raise us up, together with all who believe, and take us to live with Him forever in heaven.

See You Later / Philippians 3:20–21

Rosa's grandfather died. He was 81 years old, but he had always been in good health and full of energy. When he had knee surgery, he developed some complications. As time went on, he got sicker and sicker, and the doctors discovered more and more problems.

Rosa loved her grandpa very much, and she prayed and prayed that God would make him better. Eventually, however, Rosa realized that God's answer to her prayers was that He had a different plan. It was God's will that Grandpa would go to heaven. Then she thought about it some more. Grandpa would be in heaven. As much as she loved him and wanted to spend more time with him here on earth, how could she not be happy for him? He was going to heaven to be with Jesus.

When Grandpa died, Rosa was very sad. She is still sad sometimes because she misses him. Rosa is comforted, though, not only by the fact that he is in heaven but also by the fact that she will see him again someday.

You may remember other people who have died and the blessings received through their lives. For Christians, death doesn't have to be a sad thing. Because of Jesus' death and resurrection, we can remember that someday *all* Christians will be in heaven, celebrating with the Lord.

Rosa didn't really get a chance to say good-bye to Grandpa, but she knows she didn't really need to. To Rosa, good-bye seems kind of final. What she really would have liked to say to her grandpa was, "See you later." Rosa will see him again in heaven someday! Because of Christ, we never, even in death, have to truly say good-bye to fellow Christians. Because of Christ, we always have the privilege of saying, "See you later!"

Talk about it: What does it mean to you to know that Jesus has overcome death?

Prayer: Dear Jesus, thank You for giving me the gift of eternal life through Your death and resurrection. Comfort me when I have to deal with earthly death. Help me remember that I will see You and all Christians in heaven someday. Amen.

The Lord watch between you and me, when we are out of one another's sight. Genesis 31:49

A New Home for Abraham's Family

Genesis 13:1–14:16

God called Abraham to leave his people and go to a new home in a new land. Abraham obeyed God. Traveling with Abraham in search of a new home were Abraham's wife, Sarah, his nephew Lot, and all their animals and goods.

Because both Abraham and Lot had many flocks and herds, there began to be trouble between those who took care of Abraham's animals and those who took care of Lot's animals. Abraham said to Lot, "Look at all the land. Let's separate from each other. Choose the land you would like, and move in that direction. If you go to the right, I will move to the left. If you choose the land on the left, I will go to the right."

Lot looked out and saw the rich, well-watered Jordan River valley. He chose to move there. Abraham went and settled in the other direction. But the two remained close friends.

Once, when enemies captured Lot and his neighbors, Abraham and his servants formed an army and rescued them.

Family and friends are among God's great gifts. Sometimes, they move away from each other. But that doesn't mean they can't be close, even though they no longer live in the same place.

Jesus, our greatest friend, will always remain with us. He promises never to leave us. He promises always to remain close to us, even when other good friends may move away.

I Set You Apart / Jeremiah 1:5

While Jenny lived in Colorado, she knew who she was. She had an identity. She was the principal's kid, the blonde girl who played basketball and tennis and loved art. Friends knew her and needed her. When Jenny's family moved to California, she had to go to a new school and a new church. Nobody knew Jenny or needed her. Nobody appreciated her talents and skills. Jenny felt alone and unimportant, even though there were many other kids around her. She had lost her identity. She missed her friends.

In the Bible, God said to His prophet Jeremiah, "Before I formed you in the womb I knew you, and before you were born I consecrated you [set you apart]." Even before Jeremiah was born, God loved him and gave him some special talents. God had chosen Jeremiah to be His prophet. Jeremiah would tell God's message of judgment and of love to His people.

God made each of us. He knew us before we were born. He gave each of us a very special identity. Not only did He create us, but He also redeemed us through the life, death, and resurrection of Jesus. Through Baptism, God made us His children. With this new identity, God helps us use the special gifts He gives us to spread the message of His love and forgiveness wherever we may go or live—just as He did for Jeremiah.

As time went on, God showed Jenny her new identity in California. It really wasn't much different from her identity in Colorado. She was still a blonde, sports-loving, artistic daughter. She was still God's forgiven child, able to share with others the new identity He had given her in Jesus. She was able to remain friends with those she knew in Colorado. Plus, she made lots of new friends in California too.

Talk about it: What is important for those who love Jesus to remember when they or their loved ones move away? List your talents. Pray that the Lord will use these special gifts for His glory wherever you live.

Prayer: Lord, thank You for loving me and for going with me wherever I may go. Help me to share Your plan of love and salvation with the people in my life. Amen.

For as in one body we have many members . . . so we, though many, are one body in Christ. Romans 12:4–5

A Woman Named Ruth | Ruth 1–4

During a time of famine, a couple named Elimelech and Naomi left their home in Bethlehem and went to live in the land of Moab, together with their two sons. Soon after, Elimelech died. Each of the sons married Moabite women, and then both sons died.

Their mother, Naomi, and their wives, Ruth and Orpah, were very sad. Naomi decided to return to her home in Bethlehem. Ruth and Orpah planned to go with her, but Naomi encouraged them to stay in their homeland of Moab.

Orpah returned to her family, but Ruth refused to leave her mother-in-law. The two women traveled to Bethlehem. Ruth supported herself and Naomi by gathering the grain the farmers left behind in the fields. A man named Boaz owned one of the fields where Ruth gathered grain. Boaz was kind to Ruth because he had heard of her kindness to Naomi.

Boaz married Ruth, and God gave them a son whom they named Obed. Obed would be the grandfather of King David. Many years later, Jesus, our Savior, was born as one of Ruth's descendants.

Ruth and Naomi both loved and served the one true God. Eventually, the Savior of the world was born into their family. Like all families, the size of Ruth's family changed many times during Ruth's life. But whether Ruth's family was small or large, Ruth knew that God was with her wherever she went. And she found strength and encouragement in the life she shared with other believers.

Keeping Close / Hebrews 10:25

The cold evening air sent a chill through Robert, and he realized he was shivering. He and Dad decided to build a fire. They began to stack logs in the fireplace.

"Why can't we go to the game tomorrow?" Robert asked as they worked. "Why do we have to go to church, anyway?"

Dad was silent as he lit a match and held it to the logs. When the first flames appeared, Robert fanned them with the bellows. Soon, the fire's cozy warmth flooded the den. Robert watched the logs glow orange and crackle.

"Christians are like logs on a fire," Dad said quietly. "When we are gathered together around God's Word and Sacraments, the Holy Spirit fans our faith, and we burn brightly for God. We share the warmth of God's love for us as He feeds us with the gifts of His goodness. We grow stronger as we learn and work together. Most important, we shine God's light into a world darkened with sin when we tell others how Jesus came to be our Savior."

Dad paused as the logs shifted in the fireplace. One log rolled off the stack. Away from the flame, the log's orange glow faded quickly and the log cooled.

"When we are away from our family and other believers, our faith may cool," said Dad. "We may begin to ignore God's Word or to become confused about what it says. We no longer see our own sin. We no longer see our need for God's forgiveness in Christ. But at family devotions and in church, God surrounds us with other believers who help and encourage us. At church, God helps us see and confess our sins, and He gives us His gifts of grace and salvation to keep our faith burning brightly."

Robert understood his father's words. He didn't want His faith to cool. Maybe there was a way to do both—go to church early and get to the game late. Maybe he could set priorities—putting God first.

Attending church every week is not meant to be a burden or an annoyance. Church is a blessing. Here, God keeps our faith strong through His Word and the Sacrament. Here, we worship and enjoy the company of fellow Christians.

Talk about it: How does knowing Jesus is your Savior help you when you are feeling alone? How has your family been a blessing to you? How has your church been a blessing to you?

Prayer: Heavenly Father, thank You for Jesus, my Savior. Thank You for the family You have given me and for the blessing of belonging to a family of believers. Thank you for giving me the opportunity to warm my faith as I gather with others around Your Word and enjoy together the blessings of knowing You and Your love for us. In Jesus' name I pray. Amen.

The Lost Son | Luke 15:11–24

When we confess our sins to God, He forgives us for Jesus' sake. When Jesus forgives us, it's as if we are at the beginning of a new day. We can feel happy knowing Jesus will help us face all that will happen in the new day ahead.

Jesus once told a story to show people what God's forgiveness is like. Jesus told of a man who had two sons. The younger son asked his dad for his inheritance so that he could go out on his own. The father gave the son what he had asked for, and the son set out and went to live in a faraway land. Here, he spent all of his money on wild living. He made friends in this new place, but they were interested only in the young man's money. They were not true friends.

When his money was gone, the young man had no place to go and no way to make a living. Finally, a farmer hired him to take care of his pigs. As the young man cared for the pigs, he was so hungry that even the food the pigs were eating looked good to him. Then he remembered how well his father's servants lived. They always had plenty to eat. The young man decided that he would go back to his father. Knowing he was no longer worthy to be treated as his father's son, he would ask his father if he could work for him as a servant.

When the son was still a long way off, the father recognized his returning son and ran to meet him. The father dressed the returning son in a royal robe and put a ring on his hand and shoes on his feet. The father not only treated the young man as his son, but he also gave him a party. The father wanted to celebrate. For him, it was as if his son was dead but was now alive, was lost but now was found. For the son, as for each of us who receives Jesus' forgiveness, a new day had begun.

Something Important / 1 Thessalonians 5:16–18

Mika's mother woke her in plenty of time to get ready for school. Mika showered, dressed, ate breakfast, made her bed, and carried her backpack to the door.

I'm forgetting something, she thought. Boomer, her big gray cat, brushed her legs. She bent down to scratch his head. When Mika started to open the door, Boomer blocker her way.

"Oops, I forgot to feed you!" she said. She hurried to the laundry room and washed Boomer's tray. Then she gave him fresh food and water.

I'm still forgetting something, Mika thought. Then she remembered. She went back to her room and knelt by the bed.

"Dear Lord, forgive me for forgetting to pray. Thank You for this day and all other good things. Be with me and keep me safe. Help me share Your love with everyone I see. Amen."

Now Mika knew she was completely ready.

Sometimes, we pay too much attention to getting things done. We forget to give God time in our lives. How could we forget Jesus, the one who died for our sins? We may not like to admit it, but sometimes we push Him to the back of our minds and forget to pray.

Prayer is our chance to talk to God. We praise Him, thank Him, ask His forgiveness, and tell Him what we need. We do not have to kneel down or fold our hands. But God wants us to pray often.

There is no better way to begin each day than to talk with God. Confess your sins to Him. Bask in the joy of the forgiveness Jesus has earned for you. Then go happily into your day, knowing that your Creator, Savior, and best and truest Friend goes with you into all that the new day holds for you.

~~~~~~~~~~

Talk about it: Lamentations 3:22–23 reminds us that "the steadfast love of the Lord never ceases; His mercies never come to an end; they are new every morning." What do these words mean to you?

Prayer: Dear Father in heaven, let me always remember to honor You. Thank You for all You have given me, especially my Savior, Jesus. Help me to begin each day talking with You. Forgive my sins, and help me to live for You each new day. In the name of Jesus I pray. Amen.

I am not worthy of the least of all the deeds of steadfast love and all the faithfulness that You have shown to Your servant. Genesis 32:10

Samuel Anoints David as King | 1 Samuel 16:1–13

A baby boy was born to a man and woman who lived long ago. They thanked the true God for the gift of this son, whom they named David. He wasn't their first son, but he turned out to be the last son born to the couple.

God had a plan for this baby, as God has for every new life. As he grew, David did many of the jobs that his older brothers didn't want to do or felt they had outgrown. David often took care of the sheep, for example.

God had given David some special abilities. The Bible tells us that David could play music well. He was also brave, he spoke well, and he had a pleasing appearance. Most important, God was with David.

After Saul, Israel's first king, fell away from God, God sent the prophet Samuel to select the next king from David's family. David's father, Jesse, had all his sons pass before Samuel. When Samuel saw David's brother Eliab, he thought, "Surely this one is the Lord's anointed." But God told Samuel, "Do not look on his appearance or on the height of his stature, because I have rejected him. For the LORD sees not as man sees: man looks on the outward appearance, but the LORD looks on the heart."

After all the brothers had passed before Samuel, he asked Jesse if he had other sons. Jesse said, "There remains the youngest, but he is keeping the sheep." Jesse sent for David, and when David appeared, God indicated to Samuel that this young boy was to be anointed the next king of Israel. Samuel anointed David, and God's Spirit rushed upon David.

God chose David. And God has chosen each of us to be His people. He wants us believe in Jesus as our Savior and to receive the forgiveness Jesus came to earn for us. He wants us to live for Him. God wants us to know that He has a plan for us, a plan for our welfare and to give us a hope and future in Jesus. These are the things that can give us special joy with each birthday we celebrate.

Pretty Packages / 1 Corinthians 12:7–11

Happy birthday, Danielle; happy birthday to you." As soon as her friends stopped singing, Danielle blew out the candles on her cake.

"Open my present first!" was the shout from several people at the same time.

Danielle selected a brightly wrapped gift with a purple bow. She knew it was from Jan, her best friend. It would be something only she would know to give. Danielle carefully unwrapped the box and peeked inside. She looked up and gave Jan a big smile as she unfolded a purple shirt. It was the shirt she had shown to Jan on a recent trip to the mall.

"Thank you, Jan," she said. "It's just what I wanted. Purple is my favorite color."

Isn't it fun and exciting to have presents to open? Did you know that God has given you a special gift through the Holy Spirit? He gives each Christian a particular gift or gifts so that we can serve God in the way He has planned. Our gifts don't come brightly packaged with purple bows on top. Some of us have to search and look deep into ourselves for our special gifts.

You may have the gift of wisdom so that you can see God's plan at work in your life and the lives of others. Through the gift of faith, you can help others know Jesus. You can tell them that He is the one way to God and that He saved us by giving His life for us.

There are many kinds of gifts. Are you able to make friends feel better about a bad grade or a lost dog by talking and praying with them? Maybe, out of concern for others, you pray that God will make a sick person better, and He answers yes to your prayer. There are many other gifts. If you don't know what yours is, ask the Lord to help you discover it and use it for His glory and the good of others.

Talk about it: What kinds of abilities has God given to you? What plans do you think God may have for your future?

Prayer: Heavenly Father, thank You for another year of life. Jesus, please forgive my sins and remind me daily of Your love and care for me. Holy Spirit, please help me find and use Your gifts to give You glory and for the good of others. I pray in Jesus' name. Amen.

The eyes of all look to You, and You give them their food in due season. You open Your hand; You satisfy the desire of every living thing. Psalm 145:15–16

Jesus Feeds Thousands | Matthew 14:13–21; 15:32–39

Jesus felt compassion for the people because they were like sheep without a shepherd. He welcomed them, spoke to them about the kingdom of God, and healed many of them. When the day was nearly over, Jesus' disciples came to Him, saying, "Send the people away so that they can go into the nearby towns and villages and buy themselves something to eat, for they have nothing."

But Jesus replied, "They don't need to go anywhere. You give them something to eat."

Then Andrew, Peter's brother, said to Jesus, "There is a boy here who has five barley loaves and two small fish. But what is this little bit among so many people?"

Jesus commanded that the people sit down in groups on the grass. They sat down in groups of

hundreds and fifties, and they numbered about five thousand men, plus the women and children. Then Jesus took the five loaves and two small fish. He looked up to heaven, gave thanks, broke apart the loaves and fish, and gave them to the disciples. The disciples then gave the food to those who were sitting down. When everyone had enough to eat, Jesus told His disciples to gather up the leftovers so that nothing would be wasted. The leftovers filled twelve baskets!

Another time when a great crowd gathered to hear Jesus, the people faced a similar situation. This time, they had been with Jesus for three days and had nothing to eat. Some had come from a far land to learn from Jesus. Jesus asked the disciples how many loaves of bread they had. The disciples counted seven loaves. Jesus had the people sit on the grass. Then Jesus gave thanks to God and broke the loaves. He gave the bread to the disciples to place before the crowd to eat.

Another miracle took place! All four thousand of those present had all they wanted to eat. When the people had finished eating, the disciples picked up seven baskets of leftovers! Jesus thanked His heavenly Father for the food the people were about to receive. God's people today thank God too for the food He gives us each day.

Rye, Whole Wheat, or Pita? / Luke 11:3

Wheat bread, oat loaves, potato rolls, pita, banana bread, biscuits, scones, blueberry muffins, tortillas. The list of breads could go on and on, especially if you ask people from other countries to name some.

Bread is basic to the human diet. Whether spread with peanut butter and jelly or goat cheese, bread is eaten all around the world. It fills us up and gives us energy—and it tastes good.

Bread was important in Bible times too. Unleavened bread was eaten on the night of the Passover. Manna fed the Israelites in the wilderness. Jesus refused when Satan tempted Him to turn rocks into bread. Jesus used five small barley loaves to feed thousands of people.

There is a type of bread that's vital to our faith—Jesus Himself. In John 6:48, He says, "I am the bread of life." Jesus is necessary to our spiritual health and energy. When we take Him in through the Word of God, our faith grows stronger and our desire for forgiveness is satisfied.

When we sit down to eat each day and say a prayer thanking God for our food, we remember that all we have comes from God. He gives us good food to feed our bodies; He gives us Himself to feed our souls. In Jesus, we find all we will ever need!

Talk about it: In what different ways does Jesus feed us? What is your favorite food to eat?

Prayer: Thank You, Lord. All I am and have comes from You. I'm glad that You give me so many wonderful things each day. Thank You for giving me good food and for the blessings of forgiveness and salvation. Please keep my faith alive and growing. I want to live with You forever. Amen.

Even the darkness is not dark to you; the night is bright as the day, for darkness is as light with you. Psalm 139:12

God Makes a Promise | Genesis 12; 15

Sometimes, children say they are afraid of the dark. Probably the dark frightens them because when everything is dark it's not possible to see things that might be dangerous. God's Word reminds us that darkness and light are the same with God. He rules over both. He loves and cares for us whether we are awake or asleep. And God does not sleep.

Long ago, God used the nighttime sky to show Abraham how much He loved and cared for him. God had promised Abraham a large family. God promised that one of the children born into Abraham's family would be the Savior of the world. Abraham was already old, and he had no children. Yet Abraham believed God.

One night, God told Abraham to look into the sky and count the stars. There were so many stars that Abraham could not count them all. God told Abraham that he would have as many people in his family as there are stars in the sky. Eventually, this promise came true. The nation of God's people all came from Abraham's family. Jesus the Savior was also born into Abraham's family.

In another way, everyone who believes in the true God is a member of the family of Abraham. Because we believe in God, we need not fear things in the dark or in the light. We remain always in our Savior's love and care.

Held in God's Hand / Isaiah 41:10

Nighttime thunderstorms scare Claire. The crashing thunder and flashes of lightning send shivers down her back. Claire heads to her parents' room at the first sign of a storm. Snuggling under the warm blankets, with a parent on each side, gives Claire a sense of protection. To Claire, nothing feels better than that on a stormy night!

What scares you? Is it the thought of having to make friends in a new situation? Maybe performing or playing sports in front of a crowd frightens you. Could just taking a quiz or test in school make you feel scared and ready to run? Having someone nearby through the scary times sure can help. There are times, however, when we have to go it alone. Or do we? There's always someone nearby—God our heavenly Father. Going it alone doesn't happen when you're a part of God's family.

God's Word talks about the protection He gives us. In Isaiah 41, He tells us, "I will uphold you with My righteous right hand." What an awesome visual promise God gives us in this verse! God's mighty right hand is supporting us not only in times of trouble but always! Even our most frightening moments don't have to be scary at all. We are in God's hand.

Had God not sent His Son, Jesus, to pay for our sins on the cross, our lives would be filled with fear. Without Jesus' death and resurrection, we would have to pay for our own sins. Eternal death and hell would have been ours. Thanks to God's loving plan of salvation, Jesus made payment for our sin. The promise of eternal life in heaven is now ours! No other promise can give us more comfort.

When frightening times come your way, remember whose hand protects you. There will never be a moment when you have to do anything alone. God is there, and He always will be. Remember—He has you right in His hand.

~~~~~~~~~~~~~~~~~~~~

Talk about it: What kinds of things scare or frighten you? How does Jesus help you with your fears? Trace your hand on a piece of paper. Ask someone with a larger hand to trace his or her hand over your tracing. The large hand will represent God's hand. Write today's Bible verse on the page. Know that you always fit perfectly in God's hand.

Prayer: Heavenly Father, remind me of Your presence both day and night, when I am happy and with others, and when I feel scared and alone. Thank You for promising to keep me always in Your hand. I pray in Jesus' name. Amen.

Devotions That Answer Questions

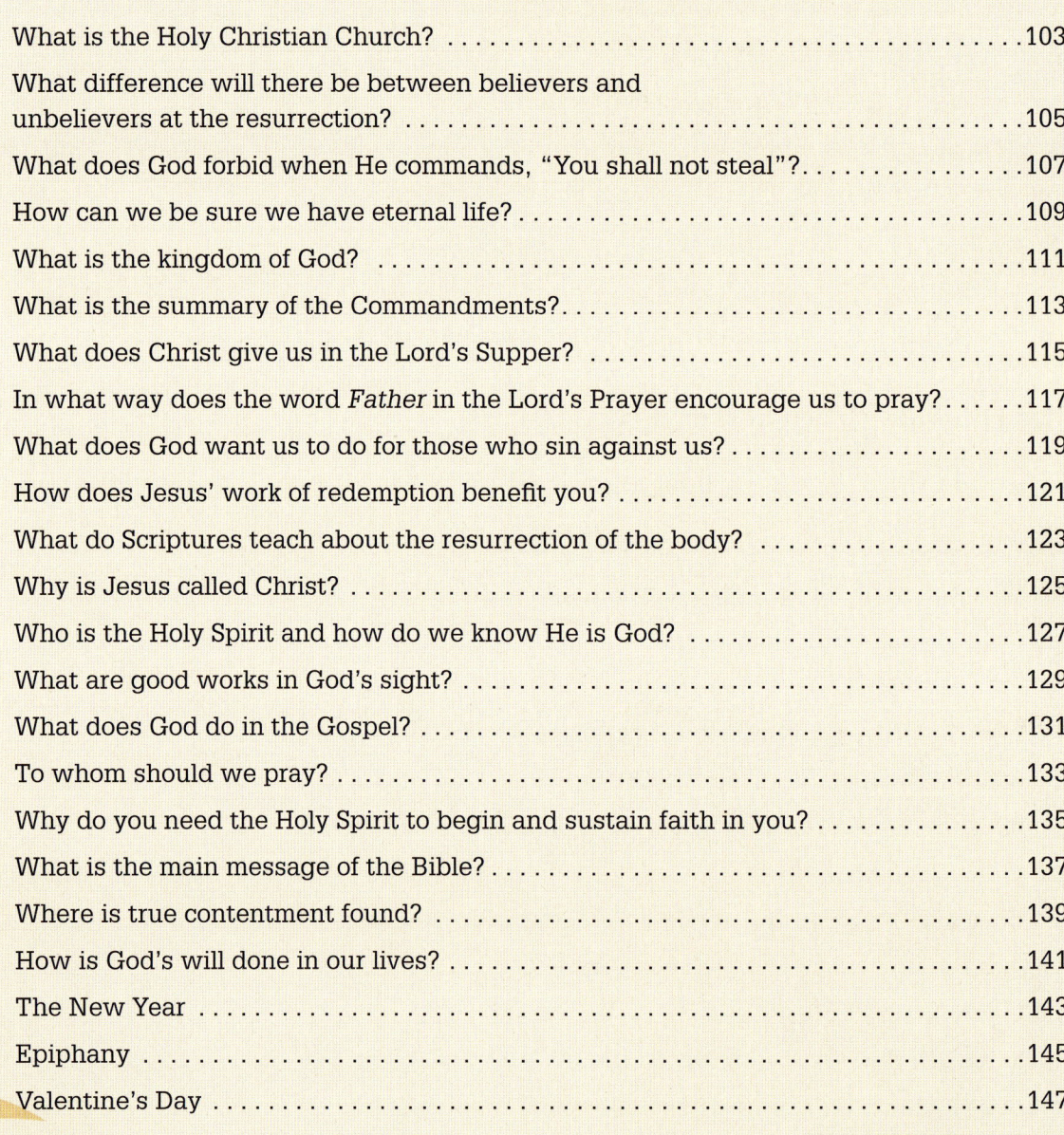

Devotions for Special Times